ISSUES THAT CONCERN YOU

Sexting

Lauri S. Scherer, *Book Editor*

GREENHAVEN PRESS

A part of Gale, Cengage Learning

GALE
CENGAGE Learning·

Detroit • New York • San Francisco • New Haven, Conn • Waterville, Maine • London

GALE
CENGAGE Learning·

Elizabeth Des Chenes, *Director, Publishing Solutions*

© 2013 Greenhaven Press, a part of Gale, Cengage Learning

Gale and Greenhaven Press are registered trademarks used herein under license.

For more information, contact:
Greenhaven Press
27500 Drake Rd.
Farmington Hills, MI 48331-3535
Or you can visit our Internet site at gale.cengage.com

Articles in Greenhaven Press anthologies are often edited for length to meet page require-ments. In addition, original titles of these works are changed to clearly present the main thesis and to explicitly indicate the author's opinion. Every effort is made to ensure that Greenhaven Press accurately reflects the original intent of the authors. Every effort has been made to trace the owners of copyrighted material.

Cover image © Aaron Amat/Shutterstock.com.

LIBRARY OF CONGRESS CATALOGING-IN-PUBLICATION DATA

Sexting / Lauri S. Scherer, book editor.
   p. cm. -- (Issues that concern you)
  Includes bibliographical references and index.
  ISBN 978-0-7377-6299-0 (hbk.)
1. Internet and teenagers. 2. Sexting. 3. Teenagers--Sexual behavior. 4. Computer sex. 5. Sexual ethics. I. Scherer, Lauri S.
  HQ799.2.I5S492 2013
  306.70285--dc23

                                      2012040005

Printed in the United States of America
2 3 4 5 6 7 17 16 15 14 13

CONTENTS

In 2012 the *Merriam-Webster's Collegiate Dictionary* added *sexting* to its collection of words, indicating how widespread the behavior had become. Reliable statistics on the number of people, and especially the number of young people, who engage in sexting remain elusive, though it is clear that sexting is an increasingly common practice—and possibly a dangerous one. Sexting has caused the breakup of marriages, the downfall of politicians, and the suicide of young people still coming to terms with their self-image and social standing. Attitudes and controversies surrounding sexting are inherently connected to society's tendency to send young people—especially girls—mixed messages about sex and sexuality.

Girls have long received conflicting messages about sex and power, and thus it may not be surprising that they report being under the most pressure to send nude, partially nude, suggestive, or sexually explicit photos of themselves. Two such girls included Jessica Logan and Hope Witsell, both of whom killed themselves after intimate photos of them ended up circulating around their schools. After succumbing to pressure to present themselves in a sexual manner, Logan and Witsell were labeled sluts and whores by other students, who taunted both girls to the edge of life. People such as Colleen Carroll Campbell of the Ethics and Public Policy Center view Logan and Witsell as not only victims of sexting and bullying but as victims of society's double standards for women and its mixed messages about sexuality. "Teens like Jessica and Hope find themselves confounded by a culture that teaches them to equate exhibitionism with empowerment, then vilifies them for the same reckless behavior it implicitly encourages,"[1] says Campbell.

Sexting's double standard was also well documented by researchers with the National Society for the Prevention of Cruelty to Children, who in 2012 conducted in-depth interviews with British teens who had experienced or participated in sexting.

An indication of how widespread and common sexting has become is the fact that Merriam-Webster added the word to the eleventh edition of its Collegiate Dictionary.

The researchers noted that sexting is accompanied by an age-old double standard for girls in which they must balance being viewed as fun and sexy against being put down as either a slut or as frigid. Girls are presented with the unfair choice of being seen as either "slags [British slang for *slut*] or drags," and are forced to put forth "just the right kind of attractive, 'sexy, but not too sexy', image."[2]

Among the many teens interviewed was Kaja, who was in the tenth grade. Kaja's comments illustrate the extent to which the girls he knows are backed into a "can't win" corner in terms of being pressured to, and then punished for, sexting. He says he thinks of girls who sext as sluts but does not think the revealing photos he posts of himself fall in this category. He also says that despite thinking of girls who sext as sluts, he is happy to accept their photos:

Kaja: [Girls who do not sext] respect [them]selves.

Interviewer: So do you think then the girls that are sending the pictures don't respect themselves then?

Kaja: They can't be respecting themselves if they are taking pictures of their body and whatever, naked.

Interviewer: What makes you say that? Could they like looking at a picture of themselves? Because you posted a picture up of your six-pack right on Facebook, what is different about it?

Kaja: That's a good question. I don't know, it's just different.

Interviewer: Different because they are a girl?

Kaja: Yeah, different because they are a girl. . . .

Interviewer: So like, does her sending you that picture that you have got there—is that like someone who doesn't respect herself do you think?

Kaja: Yeah. She don't respect herself. . . . I call any girl a slag that sends me pictures like that. Not to their face, but obviously I will know what type of girl she is.

Interviewer: So, but you like getting the picture?

Kaja: Yeah.

Interviewer: Because you kept it right? But slag is an insult?

Kaja: I know.

Interviewer: So like why would you insult something that you liked?

Kaja: But I'm not insulting her—I'm not telling her she is a slag, it is just in my head, like a slag, what type of person she is.[3]

Based on multiple comments like these, the researchers concluded, "Girls are explicitly divided into 'types' in line with well-worn sexual dichotomies. Girls are placed under pressures . . . sometimes literally bombarded with requests to send a particular boy a 'sexy' photograph of themselves. If they finally succumb to such pressure they find themselves dubbed 'slags' and put into the category of used or dirty girl."[4] Kaja's comments capture a double standard that has long challenged women, one that young girls still grappling with their sexuality and self-confidence may not yet have the tools to combat.

While parents, educators, administrators, and policy makers debate how to deter teens from sexting and what punishments are appropriate, society at large might begin to consider the ways in which long-held double standards inform the sexting phenomenon. *Issues That Concern You: Sexting* considers these and other issues through well-balanced pro/con pairs. Articles are written by a wide variety of authoritative voices that discuss the issues in ways readers will find accessible, engaging, and relevant to their lives.

Notes

1. Colleen Carroll Campbell, "'Sexting' Suicides Should Serve as Wake-up Calls," *St. Louis Dispatch*, December 10, 2009.
2. Jessica Ringrose, Rosalind Gill, Sonia Livingstone, and Laura Harvey, "A Qualitative Study of Children, Young People, and 'Sexting,'" National Society for the Prevention of Cruelty to Children, 2012. www.nspcc.org.uk/Inform/resourcesforprofes sionals/sexualabuse/sexting- research-report_wdf89269.pdf.
3. Quoted in Ringrose et al., "A Qualitative Study."
4. Quoted in Ringrose et al., "A Qualitative Study."

ONE

Adults Should Worry About Sexting

Litchfield County Times

> Editors at the *Litchfield County Times*, a Connecticut newspaper, wrote the following viewpoint, in which they argue that sexting is a serious problem about which adults should be concerned. They discuss how young people at a Connecticut high school forwarded nude pictures around the student body, wreaking havoc on students' lives. Participating in sexting destroys a young person's confidence and can forever change the course of his or her life, they warn. Sexting is so dangerous, in fact, the editors liken it to playing with loaded guns: In an instant, it can ruin one's privacy, reputation, and make one the target of cruel and unrelenting gossip. The editors urge parents to take all measures necessary—including confiscating cell phones at night—and for school officials to be on the lookout for signs of this destructive trend.

We can all remember those long ago days when the first nervous fluttering of adolescence revealed the wonders of the opposite sex to us, but until only a few years ago the perils confronting newly minted teenagers were more clearly defined. Before the days of the Internet, before the era of cell phones that can transmit pictures from anywhere in an instant, before telephone numbers rang through only to the holder of [a] cell phone, parents had a greater chance of knowing something about what was going on in their children's lives.

The Problem with Technological Freedom

It is not a new problem—a century ago, when bicycles first became a popular and readily available means of conveyance, parents gazed with dismay at the departing backs of young people who were suddenly free to move away from the oversight of their elders. Those loosened bonds quickly morphed into the ubiquitous automobile that gave young people even more mobility and privacy to pursue their personal relationships.

Technology now has taken a leap forward the equivalent of several light years, and communications among the young no longer need be conducted under a parent's or chaperone's eyes—indeed, physical proximity is not required even by the participants.

That freedom provides opportunities for children to explore their own personal development among their peers, but it also exposes them to unseen dangers that they are not mature enough to understand. Students at Housatonic Valley Regional High School in Falls Village [Connecticut] recently learned a valuable lesson about the hazards of "sexting" when correspondence between students went viral through the school. Photographs were forwarded from the original parties to other students throughout the school, causing distress to those for whom the images represented an unwelcome intrusion into their lives.

Sexting Destroys Lives

The school responded admirably to the situation. As the "buzz" reached teachers' ears, the faculty broke into their regularly scheduled classes to moderate classroom discussions about the issue and the problems that can result from thoughtless electronic transmissions. The school quickly went beyond this intervention to plan class-wide programs with community educators and with Lt. David Rice of the State Police Troop B barracks in Canaan, an officer familiar with cybercrimes. While Lieutenant Rice advised

Sexting is more common among older teens, but has been documented among children as young as eleven years old.

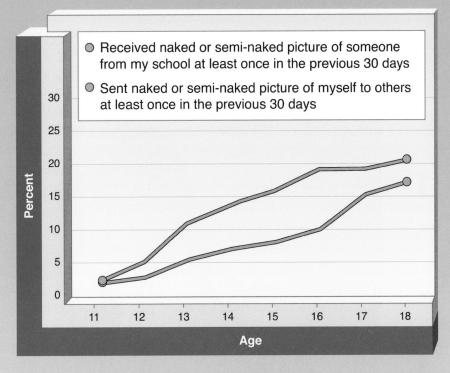

Taken from: Smeer Hinduja and Justin Patchin. "Sexting: a Brief Guide for Educators." Cyberbullying Research Center, 2010.

the students about the potential legal implications of receiving and transmitting such images—it is a Class A misdemeanor for children ages 13 to 17 to be involved in this activity and a felony for anyone older—the community educators from Housatonic Youth Service Bureau and the Women's Support Services in Sharon talked with them about the social and emotional consequences.

It was a good start, and the faculty and administration remain alert to the problem even now, when the students have moved on from the drama to other issues in their lives. But sexting can be every bit as destructive to modern children as playing with loaded guns. Because privacy can never be assumed once an image or message is launched into cyberspace, and because interpersonal relationships that grow during the budding sexuality of adolescence are notoriously unstable, it should always be assumed that

The viewpoint's authors argue that sexting is like playing with a loaded gun; it can devastate a young person's life in seconds, changing it forever.

the world will one day, even years later, be invited to share in moments that were meant to be private. Teenagers notoriously feel invulnerable, but this is not the kind of immortality they envisioned.

Our Children Need Our Protection

The sense of privacy and isolation that cell phone, iPad or computer communications engender is illusory at best. Even techno-savvy children, so proficient with navigating cyberspace, are apt to be seduced by the sense that they are alone with the person receiving their messages and pictures. But privacy, as it has been experienced in the past, is dead.

So what is a parent to do? Perhaps the most difficult thing in any relationship: they must communicate. Not on a phone, not via e-mail, but face to face. They must set standards and stick to them. They must monitor what is going on in the technological world of their young and, if necessary, collect cell phones in the evening. If they learn of any instance of sexting in their child's life, they must act quickly to address the behavior to lessen legal exposure.

It is a brave new world out there and it will take brave—and vigilant—parents to guide their young people through it. They must learn what avenues are open to them and then act consistently to protect their children.

TWO

Adults Overreact to Sexting

Paul Rapoport

The problem of teen sexting has been overblown, argues Paul Rapoport in the following viewpoint. He discusses how officials in Canada have overreacted to the few incidents of teen sexting there. In Rapoport's opinion, making extreme and unjustified warnings about sexting shames teens about their bodies and makes them unnecessarily nervous and insecure. Furthermore, many of the most dire warnings about teen sexting are simply untrue: Rapoport says that teen sexting rarely constitutes a true crime, and nude pictures of teens almost never fall into the hands of sex offenders or end up on the Internet, as adults often warn. Alarmism about sexting serves no one, concludes Rapoport: Adults would best serve teens by keeping a calmer and cooler head on the issue.

Rapoport is a professor at McMaster University in Hamilton, Ontario, and a member of the Society for the Scientific Study of Sexuality.

Sexting: is it the new bane of parenting and new test for teens? Taking a nude photo and sending it to someone has never been easier, now that cellphone cameras and email transmission are so good.

Canadian media haven't said much about sexting. Recently, however, there was an eruption of it in Cape Breton, N.S. [Nova Scotia.] In no time, the police were all over it. This was one officer's warning to parents of teens: "Taking naked photographs of anyone under the age of 18—even themselves—constitutes making child pornography." Really? Forget about teens; it's time to destroy those cute photos of your baby in the bath.

That police statement was followed by another: "Any image showing a person under the age of 18 exposing his or her breasts, sexual organs, or anal region is considered child pornography." That's a reference to the Criminal Code section on child porn. Funny, though: the Code says nothing about breasts and doesn't seem to forbid photos of shirts vs. skins soccer games.

The Problem with Sexting Alarmism

The problem with such pronouncements, which the media often glom onto, isn't just sloppy wording. If all nudity in a photo of a minor is pornographic, there are countless books

and magazines, many in libraries, that are suddenly unlawful. Some include work by famous photographers like Sally Mann and Frank Cordelle.

Alarmist warnings about sexting both reflect and promote a moral panic over children's nudity that's supposed to help them

The authors argue that adults overreact to sexting, noting that years of research have failed to show that sexy or nude photos cause an increase in sex crimes.

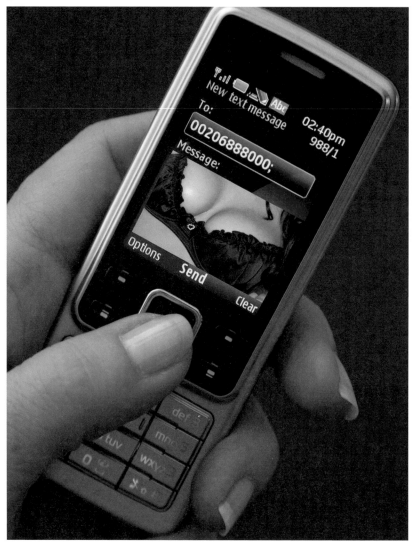

but does the opposite. They disrupt lives and increase anxiety, already prevalent in teens, in shaming them about their bodies. Child pornography is a serious matter; but how do we protect children from abusers by declaring them to be one? What's the logic that says a child is simultaneously victim and perpetrator? Child porn laws weren't meant to apply to sexting but to people abusing children for their own gratification.

The panic increases when police officers harangue, as one did in Cape Breton, about "perverts" getting hold of teens' nude photos, then lying in wait outside their homes. We may as well forbid teens to drive because someone will steal their car. Child sexual abusers are almost always known to their victims; threatening "stranger danger" over a photo is very unwise.

Sexting Has Been Exaggerated

Another reason for demoting that danger is a lack of overall effect of photos of nudity on sex crime. Apart from examples illegal in themselves, 40 years of research have failed to show that nude photos, even pornographic ones, cause or increase such crime. In 1993, the FBI concurred.

May sexting photos be illegal in themselves? Sure. Are they all? No, because nudity doesn't imply pornography, or even "sexually explicit" activity.

What about the spread of these photos on the Internet? The Crimes against Children Research Center (CCRC, in the U.S.) has shown that very few end up there. But sexting itself is an epidemic, right? Wrong. The CCRC indicates involvement of a very small percentage of teens, far under the 20 per cent figure coming from faulty research reported in 2008. (As for child sexual abuse, another purported epidemic, between 1992 and 2009 it dropped a substantial 61 per cent in the U.S. Comparable Canadian figures aren't available.)

Stop Sounding False Alarms

We should not take sexting lightly. Some people don't want to receive such photos, and the potential for bullying, coercive, and other exploitative behaviour is obvious to adults. How about explaining all that to teens and hearing their reaction? Why not start by asking them what their sexting is about? Their voices are absent from these investigations, except in the CCRC's and similar research.

Sexting may connect to personal expression or courtship. It may be a joke. Whatever it is, berating teens for it with nonsense thwarts the possibility of honest, safe, helpful discussion of teen sexuality.

The Cape Breton police have laid no charges—yet. But law enforcement should attend to sexting only in instances of exploitation or other real crimes. The solution to this problem lies with parents and other responsible adults in a process of education, not in repeated false alarms from the Chicken Littles of the sexual disaster brigades.

THREE

Considerable Numbers of Teens Engage in Sexting

Todd Ackerman

Todd Ackerman is a journalist with the *San Antonio News Express*, a Texas newspaper. In the following viewpoint he discusses evidence that shows more than one in four teens have sent sexually explicit photographs of themselves via their cell phones; more than half have been asked to send such photos. Ackerman says that this is many more teens than were previously thought to engage in sexting. One reason the survey yielded higher results is because it relied on private questionnaires, which perhaps allowed students to answer questions more honestly than other studies, which used phone surveys (teens might be more reluctant to truthfully answer questions about sexting when their parents are in earshot). Ackerman concludes that sexting is as common as parents fear and can have dire consequences in a young person's life.

Parents beware: Chances are greater than one in four that your teenager is texting naked self-portraits, according to a new study.

In the large survey of Houston-area high schools published Monday, 28 percent of both boys and girls said they had sent sexually explicit photographs of themselves with their mobile devices, a practice known as "sexting," though the vast majority of girls were bothered by requests for such images.

"This is a modern-day version of 'you show me yours, and I'll show you mine,'" said Jeff Temple, the study's lead author and a psychology professor at the University of Texas Medical Branch at Galveston. "Among teenagers, sexting is as common as parents fear."

The study, published in the journal *Archives of Pediatrics & Adolescent Medicine*, found that 57 percent of the high school students had been asked to send a naked photo and that about a third had asked for a naked photo to be sent to them.

Temple said sexting has a place in marital therapy to spice things up, but he called it a cause for concern among teens. Immature people in transient relationships, he said, are more likely to circulate the photos widely and cause embarrassment and damage to reputations.

The Houston numbers would seem high for the San Antonio area, Alamo Heights Independent School District spokesman Dick Smith said, adding, "This certainly hasn't been an epidemic for us."

Smith said district officials "every now and then hear of something" but have never found evidence of sexting—though they can't rule out the possibility.

North East Independent School District has no statistics on sexting incidents among its students but takes a proactive approach, spokeswoman Aubrey Chancellor said.

The NEISD code of conduct prohibits students from using cellphones in school except for approved educational purposes, but even if kids are sexting off campus, the district will have to deal with the fallout, she said.

"Our administrators regularly have conversations with students about the consequences of doing things on the Internet, because it's going to stay with them forever, and that includes sexting," Chancellor said.

The topic is being elevated thanks to a state-required Internet safety and "digital citizenship" curriculum all schools will integrate into classes starting this fall, Smith said.

A survey of Houston-area high schools revealed that 28 percent of boys and girls said they had sent sexually explicit photographs of themselves via their mobile devices.

Temple said the most unsettling thing about the Houston study was the finding that teen girls who sexted, unlike boys, admitted to engaging in more risky sexual behaviors, including multiple partners and using drugs or alcohol before sex.

Houston young people interviewed Monday did not dispute the findings.

"It's all you hear teenagers doing," said Leslie Riascos, 17. She said she's never sexted.

The study rebuts recent claims that the phenomenon is over-blown among teens. Those claims were based on a 2011 study in the journal *Pediatrics* that found only 1 percent of minors older than 10 had taken explicit photos and that 6 percent had received such photos. The study surveyed 1,560 children and caregivers.

But Temple said that survey's random digit dialing to homes with mostly land telephone lines resulted in an underestimate because such households tend to be less ethnically diverse, more conservative and of high socio-economic status. Teens might be less candid in their parents' homes answering questions about sexting, he said.

UTMB researchers distributed questionnaires to about 1,000 students in seven public high schools in four Houston-area school

Percentage of Students Reporting Having Sent or Received a Sexually Explicit Cell Phone Picture ("Sexting")

A 2012 study found that nearly 20 percent of high school students have sent a sexually explicit image of themselves, while more than 25 percent have forwarded such pictures to others. The following chart shows the breakdown of senders and recipients by grade and gender.

Year in School	Males		Females	
	Sent	Received	Sent	Received
Freshmen	9.2	38.5	14.0	25.0
Sophomores	23.3	56.7	14.0	24.0
Juniors	18.9	43.2	17.3	28.0
Seniors	26.5	65.1	24.2	46.2
Mean	**18.3**	**49.7**	**17.3**	**30.9**

Taken from: Donald S. Strassberg et al. "Sexting by High School Students: An Exploratory and Descriptive Study." *Archives of Sexual Behavior*, June 7, 2012.

districts in spring 2010. Thirty-two percent of participants were Hispanic, 30 percent were Anglo and 27 percent were black.

The survey found that 34.5 percent of Caucasians admitted sending sexually explicit texts, compared with 27 percent of blacks and 21.5 percent of Hispanics. The older the teen, the greater the prevalence of sexting, it found: 20 percent among students 15 or younger; 45 percent among those 18 or older.

It found both boys and girls who engaged in sexting were overwhelmingly more likely to have had sex than those who had not.

Temple said pediatricians and other teen-focused health-care providers should screen for sexting behavior and use it as an opportunity to discuss sexual behavior and safe sex. He also urged parents to counsel their teen children about sexting.

The findings support efforts to soften legal penalties for juvenile sexting. Under most existing laws, Temple said, millions of teens could be prosecuted for child pornography if the findings are extrapolated nationally.

Temple said he couldn't explain why so many girls sexted even though 57 percent of them were very bothered and another 36 percent a little bothered at being asked.

FOUR

Teens Sext Much Less Often than People Think

Larry Magid

> Larry Magid is a technology journalist who writes for *Forbes*. In the following viewpoint Magid argues that teens rarely send nude photos of themselves to each other. He cites data from a study that found a slim minority of teens engage in sexting—just 1.3 percent of teens surveyed said they had texted nude photos of themselves, and only 2.5 percent said they had sent partially nude photos. Magid points out this is much lower than other studies that claim nearly 30 percent of America's teens sext. Furthermore, Magid says that when teens do sext, it is often harmless—very rarely do such photos end up on the Internet or in the hands of sexual predators. More often, sexting simply reflects typical teen impulses to flirt or sexually experiment. Magid hopes that news that teen sexting is rare will help adults discuss the issue calmly and reasonably.

A new report from the prestigious Crimes Against Children Research Center (CACRC) at the University of New Hampshire should put to rest the notion that America's children are routinely sending around naked pictures of themselves.

Yes, it happens, but it's a lot less prevalent than many people claim. A nationally representative sample of 1,560 10 to 17 year-olds found that only 1.3% had sent or created an image of themselves that showed breasts, genitals or "someone's bottom." A somewhat higher number (2.5%) sent images where they were either nude, partially nude or in a sexy pose, even if fully clothed.

David Finkelhor is the director of the Crimes Against Children Research Center, which published a study that found that sixteen- and seventeen-year-olds are far more likely to send a sext than younger kids.

A 2009 study from the National Campaign to Prevent Teen and Unplanned Pregnancy had reported that 20% of teens had engaged in sexting but this study included 18 and 19 year-old adults. A more credible recent report from the Pew Internet & American Life Project . . . put the number at 2%, but they surveyed 12 to 17 year-olds which eliminated the very low-risk 10 and 11 year old population.

The CACRC study also found that older teens are far more likely to send a sext than younger kids. More than seven in 10 (72%) of the kids who had sent nude or partially nude images were 16 or 17.

About 7% of youth had received a nude or nearly nude image in the past year, but a single image could be sent to multiple kids.

Sexting Is Usually Benign

The same researchers also published a separate study of law enforcement agencies which found that two thirds (67%) of the nearly 3,500 cases investigated by law enforcement "involved an 'aggravating' circumstance beyond the creation and/or dissemination of a sexual image. " A third of the cases (33%) were categorized as "experimental," meaning that adults weren't involved and there was no evidence of "intent to harm or reckless misuse." These images, according to the report, "appear to grow out of typical adolescent impulses to flirt, find romantic partners, experiment with sex and get attention from peers." The researchers concluded that "what has come to be called sexting, is a diverse phenomenon," ranging from "serious criminal dynamics" to "experimental romantic and sexual attention seeking among adolescents." While sexting may be new, that general type of behavior, I might add, has been going on since the beginning of recorded history.

Reassuring News About Teen Behavior

The study's lead author, Dr. Kimberly Mitchell called the results "reassuring." She added, "as a parent I think it's good news that this is not as widespread as we have been led to believe. There is

A 2012 study published in the journal *Pediatrics* reported that sexting is much rarer than many fear.

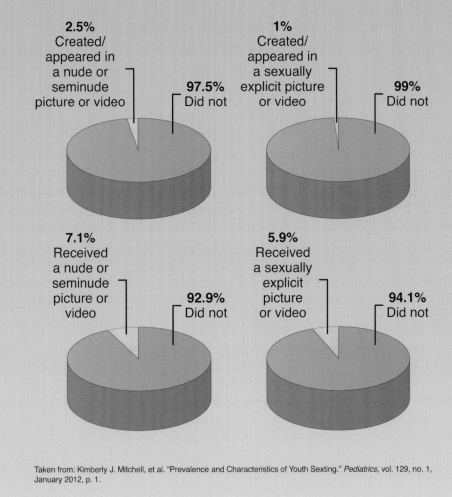

2.5%
Created/
appeared in
a nude or
seminude
picture or video

97.5%
Did not

1%
Created/
appeared in
a sexually
explicit picture
or video

99%
Did not

7.1%
Received
a nude or
seminude
picture or
video

92.9%
Did not

5.9%
Received
a sexually
explicit
picture
or video

94.1%
Did not

Taken from: Kimberly J. Mitchell, et al. "Prevalence and Characteristics of Youth Sexting." *Pediatrics*, vol. 129, no. 1, January 2012, p. 1.

this tendancy especially when it comes to kids and technology to be very alarmed with the newest thing that's out there."

Just as some people have panicked over kids who sext, others have focused on some well publicized cases where police and prosecutors over-reacted by charging kids with production, distribution or possession of child pornography, which can result in a prison sentence and being listed on a sex offender registry, perhaps for life. But the good news is that just as most kids are pretty sensible, so are most police agencies and prosecutors.

A Minority of Teens Are Affected

Sixty two percent of the cases involving adults resulted in an arrest as did 36% of the youth-only aggravated cases. But arrests were made in only 18% of the experimental cases. That's still a risk factor and one reason why, in our "Tips to Prevent Sexting, ConnectSafely.org advises parents to "consider that, while intending to protect your child, you could incriminate another—and possibly your own child." I serve as co-director of ConnectSafely.

The survey found that 21% of the kids who appeared in or created these images "reported feeling very or extremely upset," but to put that in perspective, that's 21% of 2.5% of all kids which comes to about 1 in every 200 kids. About 25% of the kids who received images were embarrassed or upset.

FIVE

There Are No Trustworthy Statistics on the Prevalence of Sexting

Kaitlin Lounsbury, Kimberly J. Mitchell, and David Finkelhor

In the following viewpoint Kaitlin Lounsbury, Kimberly J. Mitchell, and David Finkelhor argue that most studies on teen sexting are so flawed that it is impossible to know for sure the extent of the problem. They overview several major studies on teen sexting and find disturbing problems with all of them. One study, for example, polled a group of teens that did not accurately represent the teen population; the findings of another study were greatly distorted by the media. Yet another study used such loose definitions of sexting and other terms that no relevant conclusions may be drawn from it, they say. Lounsbury, Mitchell, and Finkelhor conclude there are no authoritative or accurate studies on the issue of sexting and thus the media cannot say for sure the extent of the problem.

Lounsbury, Mitchell, and Finkelhor are researchers with the Crimes Against Children Research Center, which is based at the University of New Hampshire.

The problem of teen "sexting" has captured a great deal of media attention, causing concern among parents, educators, and law enforcement officials. In reaction to these concerns, a number of studies have been conducted by researchers from many different organizations to estimate the prevalence of the problem, with widely-varying findings. This fact sheet will provide an overview of the most widely-cited studies, along with their strengths and weaknesses. . . .

An Inaccurate Study

One of the first and most commonly cited studies on sexting was conducted by the National Campaign to Prevent Teen and Unplanned Pregnancy with the help of Cosmogirl.com. The survey was conducted using an online sample of 1,280 respondents (653 teens age 13–19 and 627 young adults age 20–26).

Major Findings: 20% of teens, ages 13 to 19, including 18% of teen boys and 22% of teen girls had sent or posted nude or semi-nude pictures or videos of themselves on the Internet or through a cell phone. The majority of teens said they sent sexually suggestive content to boyfriends or girlfriends. However, 21% of teen girls and 39% of teen boys said they sent the content to someone they wanted to date or "hook up" with. Fifteen percent of teens who had sent sexually suggestive content did so to someone they only knew online.

Limitations: There are several points to keep in mind when interpreting the findings of [this] survey. First, the "teens" described in the study included 18- and 19-year-olds. It is legal for these *adults* to produce and share sexual photos of themselves. However, it is still the "20% of all teens" statistic that is most commonly cited, even though the major concern should be about sexual pictures of minors only, images that could be illegal.

Second, the participants did not constitute a representative sample, meaning that the survey results cannot be considered characteristic of the youth population in general. The teens and young adults participating in the survey had all volunteered to do multiple online surveys through a survey center called TRU.

Participants were weighted to reflect the demographic composition of the U.S. population, but the researchers admitted that the respondents did not constitute a probability sample. . . .

Finally, the definition of sexting used by these researchers ("nude or semi-nude pictures or video") could include many types of images that are not illegal under federal law. For example, "semi-nude" could include images of youth in bathing suits or underwear, which would generally not be illegal. Since the major concern is the exchange of illegal images of youth, the findings of this study do not accurately address the primary issue at hand.

Distorted Findings

Less than one year after [that] survey, Cox Communications commissioned Harris Interactive to conduct a similar study looking at teens' online and wireless safety practices. The study was conducted online and the sample included 655 teens ages 13–18 recruited online and weighted to be representative of the U.S. population of teens in that age range.

Major Findings: About one in five teens (19%) had engaged in sexting (sending, receiving, or forwarding text messages or emails with nude or nearly-nude photos) and over one-third knew of a friend who had sent or received these kinds of messages. However, only 12% of teen girls and 6% of teen boys had *sent* a "sext." . . . Only 3% of all teens in the study forwarded a sext after receiving it from someone else. Teens mainly sent the messages to boyfriends and girlfriends or someone they had a "crush" on. However, about 1 in 10 sexters said they sent these messages to people they did not know and 18% of sext receivers did not know the person who sent the messages to them.

Limitations: The statement most commonly used to summarize the findings ("one in five teens has engaged in sexting") distorts the true findings of this study. This "one in five" statistic is largely made up of teens who only received the images; only 9% actually produced and sent the messages themselves and only 3% forwarded messages. Production and distribution of sexual images are the primary concern with sexting, because these are the activities that have the highest potential to result in legal ramifications.

There are also problems with the study sample. Like the [previous] study, 18-year-olds were included in the sample, possibly distorting the findings, because sexting among these individuals would not be illegal. Cox Communications researchers did point out that 8 in 10 of the teens in their sample were under age 18, but the results were not broken down by age. Also, the sample was drawn from an online panel, which experts have advised against using for national prevalence estimates, as previously mentioned. . . .

Serious Flaws and Questionable Data

In November 2009, researchers at the South West Grid for Learning in collaboration with the University of Plymouth announced the results to date of an on-going study on sexting. The head researcher, Dr. Andy Phippen, presented his study as evidence of a "significantly larger problem than we first imagined" and later went on to say that "it is immediately apparent that such practices are cause for concern."

Major Findings: The researchers found that 40% of students knew friends who had sexted, defined as "sharing explicit images electronically." Twenty-seven percent of the students said that sexting happens regularly or "all of the time."

Limitations: A review of the research report suggests that this study should not be included in any estimates of sexting prevalence due to a number of serious flaws. First, the term "sexting" is loosely defined, as previously mentioned, as "the sharing of explicit images electronically." There was little consensus amongst the students over what "explicit" meant, with some stating that topless and nude images were acceptable and others stating that pictures of fully clothed people in public were inappropriate. Such vast differences in opinion call into question responses to the other survey questions about sexting.

Second, the researchers did not ask students if they themselves had ever produced, received, or forwarded sexual images.

Sexting Studies May Not Be Accurate

Five of the most widely cited sexting studies surveyed different populations of young people and used different definitions of sexting. Their results thus widely varied, and some claim none are authoritative.

Survey	Sample	Definition of "Sexting"
Sex & Tech Survey	653 teens age 13–19 627 young adults age 20–26	"Sent, or posted online, nude or seminude pictures or video of themselves"
Teen Online & Wireless Safety Survey	655 teens age 13–18	"Sending sexually suggestive text messages or e-mails with nude or nearly-nude photos"
AP-MTV Digital Abuse Study	1,247 young people 14–24	"Sending or forwarding nude, sexually suggestive, or explicit pics on your cell or online"
South West Grid for Learning Sexting Survey	535 students age 13–18	"The sharing of explicit images electronically" and "any of your friends shared intimate pictures/ videos with a boyfriend or girlfriend"
PEW Internet & American Life Project	800 teens age 12–17	[Sent or received] "sexually suggestive nude or nearly-nude photo or video" . . . "using your cell phone"

Taken from: Kaitlin Lounsbury et al. "The Prevalence of 'Sexting.'" Crimes Against Children Research Center. University of New Hampshire, April 2011, p. 2.

Instead, students were asked, "Have any of your friends shared intimate pictures/videos with a boyfriend or girlfriend (sometimes referred to as "sexting")?" The researchers defended this targeting of friends rather than respondents by saying they felt respondents would be more open about a friend's practices than their own. However, it is conceivable that these 40% of students could have been referring to the same small group of friends that were known by their peers to be "sexters." This would mean that only a small fraction of the students were actually producing sexual images, which should have been the main concern. . . .

Better Studies Are Needed

Recent media reports have given the impression that "sexting" is a problem of epidemic proportions among teenagers today. However, analysis of the relevant research to date reveals that there is little consistency in the estimated prevalence of sexting among adolescents. In addition, the high estimates that have

Dr. Glenda Kaufman Kantor, left, and Dr. David Finkelhor of the Crime Against Children Research Center. The center has found that most studies concerning teen sexting are so flawed that it is impossible to know for sure the extent of the problem.

received the most media attention come from studies with a number of problems including unrepresentative samples, vaguely defined terms, and great potential for public misperception. Many otherwise valid findings have been presented by the media in ways that exaggerate the true extent of the problem. While sexting does seem to occur among a notable minority of adolescents, there is little reliable evidence that the problem is as far-reaching as many media reports have suggested. Although more conservative estimates do exist, these statistics are not as widely publicized.

Changes should be made to improve future studies on this topic. First, researchers should limit samples to only include minors (age 17 or younger) if they wish to address the primary concerns about youth-produced child pornography. While it may be interesting to study sexting rates among young adults, sexual images of this population are not illegal and should not be combined with estimates of sexting among minors.

Second, terminology should be consistent among studies, accurately reported by the media, and adequately explained to youth participants. Using terms such as "nude or nearly-nude images" may confuse teens participating in the studies and result in inaccurate estimates. It would also be best to focus only on images, not written exchanges, because sexual photographs of minors are illegal; sexual text messages between youth are generally not. If researchers used this standard terminology, more meaningful comparisons could be made between studies.

It is clear that a standardized definition of sexting is needed. Although sexting has become a popular term among the public, it has come to encompass too many activities to make it an appropriate term for formal research. Instead, the authors suggest using the term "youth-produced sexual images," defined as images created by minors (age 17 or younger) that depict minors and that are or could be considered child pornography under criminal statutes.

Third, there should be a greater emphasis on who these youth are sharing sexual images with and their reasons for doing this. While most media reports focus on youth sexting among peers, some youth may be sending sexual images to people they barely know, such as people they meet online. These online recipients could be adults who are pressuring teens into taking and sending the images. Most people would likely agree that these situations deserve more police attention.

We Cannot Know the Extent of Sexting

Journalists and scholars seem eager to cite statistics about sexting, but this may be unwise due to the current lack of consistent findings and significant flaws in many studies. When citing the statistics, it is important to mention them in the context of other studies and also take into account the variety of circumstances that the term "sexting" can be used to describe. Until more reliable statistics are available, scholars and journalists should avoid citing the potentially inaccurate studies currently available. We suggest that journalists simply say: "there are no consistent and reliable findings at this time to estimate the true prevalence of the problem." At the very least, study findings should be presented in ways that do not exaggerate the problem or mislead readers. Writers should also clearly state what behaviors the statistics are referring to and not simply use the umbrella term of "sexting" to refer to the many different activities covered in the studies.

SIX

Peer Pressure Causes Sexting

Jessica Ringrose, Rosalind Gill, Sonia Livingstone, and Laura Harvey

Sexting is largely driven by peer pressure, argue Jessica Ringrose, Rosalind Gill, Sonia Livingstone, and Laura Harvey in the following viewpoint. They conducted thorough interviews with thirty-five young people in London and found that both boys and girls face enormous pressure to participate in sexting. Girls are under the most pressure to send nude photos of themselves, and face a double standard: Many are called sluts if they do text photos, and prudes if they do not. Boys, on the other hand, are under pressure to solicit such photos for fear of being labeled homosexual if they show no interest. The authors conclude that sexting is a form of sexualized bullying that can wreak havoc on a teen's academic, social, and personal life.

Ringrose is with the Institute of Education in London. Gill is with Kings College, London. Livingstone is with the London School of Economics, and Harvey is with Open University.

Given the paucity of prior research to guide us [this] study was designed to listen to young people's views and experiences rather than to test any particular conceptions of sexting. Unlike those who would restrict sexting to particular technologies or practices (notably, the peer exchange of illegal images), we aimed to scope the nature of the range of practices that young teenagers are experiencing in order to gain insight into their own understandings. Thus we began with an open mind, being ourselves undecided at the outset as to whether 'sexting' is a coherent phenomenon that constitutes 'a problem' for which policy intervention is required.

The Pressure to Sext

However, the findings did reveal some problems as experienced by young people, and we have sought to distinguish this from the headline panics in the popular press. We uncovered a great diversity of experiences, which contradicts any easy assumptions about sexting as a singular phenomenon. Nor can it simply be described in absolute terms—wanted vs. unwanted sexual activity, deliberate vs. accidental exposure—for much of young people's engagement with sexual messages and images lies in the ambiguous and grey zone. Few teenagers wish to be excluded from the sexual banter, gossip, discussion or, indeed, from the flirtatious and dating activity endemic to youth culture. But to take part is to be under pressure—look right, perform, compete, judge and be judged. Much of young peoples talk, therefore, reflects an experience that is pressurised yet voluntary—they choose to participate but they cannot choose to say 'no'. We also argue that because sexting is not just an individual practice but also a group, networked phenomenon, its effects are not limited to the actors engaged in some specific practice but permeates and influences the entire teen network in multiple ways.

The Enemy Is Each Other

For young people, the primary technology-related threat is not the 'stranger danger' hyped by the mass media but technology-mediated sexual pressure from their peers. For example, rarely did children express to us any concern about inappropriate sexual approaches from strangers (and when they did, they seemed able quickly to brush off the approach as from a 'weirdo', 'pervert' or

Few teens wish to be excluded from the sexual banter, discussion, gossip, and flirtatious behavior inherent in sexting.

'paedo' [pedophile]). Rather, the problems posed by sexting come from their peers—indeed, from their 'friends' in their social networks, thus rendering much commonplace advice (about being careful who you contact, or keeping your profile private) beside the point. The success of e-safety campaigns is evident in teenagers' awareness of practices to reduce online risk from strangers, and it is time to shift the focus towards reducing risk from known peers. This poses a challenge for school-based awareness strategies as a class is likely to contain varieties of victim, abuser and bystander simultaneously. Also challenging is the ever-widening circles of peers, more or less known, enabled by technology.

Sexting does not refer to a single activity but rather to a range of activities which may be motivated by sexual pleasure but are often coercive, linked to harassment, bullying and even violence. There is no easy line to be drawn between sexting and bullying, for instance, and much may be learned from anti-cyberbullying initiatives to address the problem of sexting. To achieve this, teachers, parents and other adults must be willing to discuss sexual matters and sexual bullying and cyberbullying with teenagers, including as part of existing anti-bullying initiatives.

Girls Are Under More Pressure than Boys

Sexting is not a gender-neutral practice; it is shaped by the gender dynamics of the peer group in which, primarily, boys harass girls, and it is exacerbated by the gendered norms of popular culture, family and school that fail to recognise the problem or to support girls. We found considerable evidence of an age-old double standard, by which sexually active boys are to be admired and 'rated', while sexually active girls are denigrated and despised as 'sluts'. This creates gender specific risks where girls are unable to openly speak about sexual activities and practices, while boys are at risk of peer exclusion if they do not brag about sexual experiences. It is important that safety initiatives provide gender sensitive support for girls without treating sexting as a girl-only or girl-initiated problem; the role, responsibility and experiences of boys in relation to sexting also deserve more research and practical attention.

Technology is not neutral either: the specific features or affordances of mobile phones, social networking sites and other communication technologies facilitate the objectification of girls via the creation, exchange, collection, ranking and display of images. Technology providers should do more to provide easy-to-use, age-appropriate tools by which children and young people can avoid, reduce or seek redress for distress resulting from the creation, circulation and display of unwanted sexual images and text.

Sexting Reveals Wider Sexual Pressures

Although the extent of sexting cannot be determined from a small-scale qualitative study, most children interviewed were familiar with the practices referred to as sexting; while some had experienced or knew of others who had experienced sexting, also important was the finding that most felt in some ways oppressed by perceived sexual pressure—to perform, judge and be judged—from peers. Such pressures may vary by context, but the specificity of sexualisation pressures—e.g. expectations on appearance (being very thin, having large breasts or big muscles) or actions (viewing porn, tripping and touching up, performing blow jobs, sending images of own body parts)—should be discussed in order to undermine the culture of silence that further harms youth, especially girls.

It is striking that although the year 10 teenagers interviewed were more sexually aware and experienced, with many stories to tell regarding their own/their peers' sexual and sexting activities, they also appeared more mature in their resilience and ability to cope. The year 8 children were more worried, confused and, in some cases, upset by the sexual and sexting pressures they face, and their very youth meant that parents, teachers and others did not support them sufficiently. It is unknown whether sexting affects still younger children but we recommend that research and policy initiatives are developed to look at primary children and transitions into secondary school.

The Pressure to Perform

New technologies enable public displays of identity, which bring with them pleasures but also pressures to perform particular idealised forms of femininities and masculinities which are culturally, class and 'race' specific. Young people are also, however,

Teens Feel Pressure to Participate in Sexting

A 2011 survey taken jointly by MTV an the Associated Press found that significant numbers of teens are sending sexually explicit images of themselves to others, and many because they feel pressure to do so.

Question: Have you ever used your cell phone or the Internet to send naked pictures of yourself or someone else?

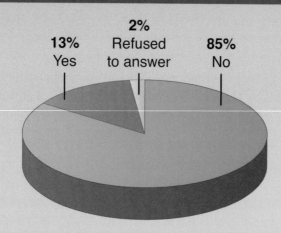

13%
Yes

2%
Refused
to answer

85%
No

Question: Were you pressured by someone to send naked pictures or videos of yourself?

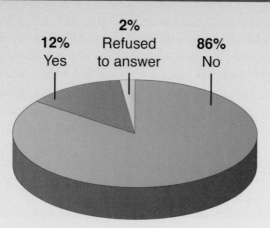

12%
Yes

2%
Refused
to answer

86%
No

Taken from: MTV–Associated Press. "Digital Abuse Survey," September 2, 2011, p. 29.

managing globalised consumer oriented cultures of consumption, which present challenges and pressures to have the 'right' types of embodiment, commodities, and status symbols. Sexting for girls can involve being subject to oppressive, racialised beauty norms and hierarchies around feminine appearance and body ideals. Boys must negotiate competitive masculinity, where status can be generated in new ways via technology (such as soliciting, collecting and distributing peer-produced sexualised images of girls' bodies, which operate as a form of commodity or currency). It follows resources need to link sexting practices to an analysis of wider sexist gender relations and commercial culture, but also address the locally specific peer based forms that sexting takes.

To overcome the culture of silence, adult embarrassment, and a paralysing uncertainty over changing sexual norms, the adults who variously provide for youth—teachers, parents, industry, commerce and others—should develop an explicit discourse that recognises, critiques and redresses the gendered sexual pressures on youth. Sexting may only reveal the tip of the iceberg in terms of these unequal and often coercive sexual pressures, but they also make such pressures visible, available for discussion and so potentially open to resolution.

SEVEN

Primal Exhibitionism Causes Sexting

Ogi Ogas

> In the following viewpoint Ogi Ogas argues that sexting is driven by a primal human urge to display oneself. He explains that male monkeys display their genitalia to prospective mates, and also to communicate their power to other males. Ogas says the tendency of men to sext photos of their private parts stems from the same desire: to indicate their sexual interest and prowess. Women's interest in sexting has deep biological roots too, says Ogas, but these are slightly different: Women have a primal urge to be desired by the opposite sex, and thus for centuries have displayed themselves when the opportunity arises. Ogas concludes that humans are hardwired for exhibitionism, and new technologies perfectly play into this primal, biological urge.
>
> Ogas is a cognitive neuroscientist and coauthor of the 2011 book *A Billion Wicked Thoughts: What the World's Largest Experiment Reveals About Human Desire*.

Over the past two years, more photographs of bare-naked celebrity anatomy have been leaked to the public eye than over the previous two centuries: Scarlett Johansson snapping a blurry self-portrait while sprawled on her bed, Vanessa Hudgens posing for a cellphone in a bracelet and a smile, Congressman [Anthony]

Wiener touting a Blackberry and a mirror in the House Members Gym, [actress] Jessica Alba, [singer] Christina Aguilera, [actress and singer] Miley Cyrus, [basketball player] Ron Artest, [actress] Charlize Theron, [recording artist] Chris Brown, [football player] Bret Favre, [and musical artists] Rihanna, Pete Wentz, Ke$ha, and dozens more.

This flood of celebrity skin has prompted folks to wonder, 'Why are so many famous people exhibitionists?' The source of all this *au naturel* flaunting lies not in the culture of fame, but in the design of our sexual brains. In fact, research has unveiled two distinct explanations: Female exhibitionism appears to be primarily cortical, while male exhibitionism is mainly subcortical.

The Desire to Be Desired

"The desire of the man is for the woman," [19th-century author] Madame de Stael famously penned, "The desire of the woman is for the desire of the man." Being the center of sexual attention is a fundamental female turn-on dramatized in women's fantasies, female-authored erotica, and in the cross-cultural gush of sultry self-portraits.

Studies have found that more than half of women's sexual fantasies reflect the desire to be sexually irresistible. In one academic survey, 47 percent of women reported the fantasy of seeing themselves as a striptease dancer, harem girl, or other performer. Fifty percent fantasized about delighting many men.

"Being desired is very arousing to women," observes clinical psychologist Marta Meana, president of the Society for Sex Therapy and Research. "An increasing body of data is indicating that the way women feel about themselves may be very important to their experience of sexual desire and subjective arousal, possibly even outweighing the impact of their partners' view of them."

Not Just Celebrities

The desire to be desired drives young women's willingness to enter wet T-shirt contests and flash what their mama gave them at Mardi Gras. Whereas male exhibitionism is considered a psychiatric disorder and sometimes a crime, female exhibitionism is rarely

What Do Teens Sext Pictures Of?

A 2012 study published in the journal *Pediatrics* reported that sexted pictures often feature graphic images that were sometimes taken as the result of trickery, drug use, or without a person's knowledge.

Characteristics of Nude or Nearly Nude Images or Videos of Minors*

Characteristics	Respondent appeared in or created image %	Respondent received image %
Pictures showed breasts, genitals, or someone's bottom		
Yes	54%	84%
Naked breasts	31%	63%
Genitals	36%	56%
Someone mooning camera	10%	15%
Someone's bottom (not mooning)	21%	28%
Someone completely nude	26%	53%
Sexual intercourse	0%	5%
Masturbation	10%	13%
Some other sexual contact	0%	9%
No or don't know/not ascertainable	46%	16%
Kids wearing underwear	31%	10%
Kids wearing bathing suits	18%	8%
Focused on private parts but clothed	10%	5%
Sexy poses with clothes on	23%	9%
Aggravating features		
Kids under influence of alcohol or drugs	13%	8%
Violence	3%	1%
Trickery or deception	3%	3%
Without person's knowledge	8%	7%
Against will	5%	1%
Money exchanged	3%	0%
Other promises or gifts	10%	3%
Any of the above	31%	15%

*Answers do not total 100% because respondents could select multiple answers.

Taken from: Kimberly J. Mitchell, et al. "Prevalence and Characteristics of Youth Sexting: A National Study." *Pediatrics*, vol. 129, no. 1, January 2012, p. 6.

considered a social problem. Just the opposite: It's exploited commercially. Multi-millionaire Joe Francis built his Girls Gone Wild empire by taping college girls stripping down for his no-budget camera crew. How does he persuade young women to disrobe? He offers them a T-Shirt and a chance to be ogled by millions of men.

"Look I'm human, & just like every girl in this world, I admire my body so i take pics," wrote singer Teyana Taylor after her graphic self-portraits were leaked. International data supports Taylor's contention that the female exhibitionist urge is universal. In Brazil, Japan, Ghana, and the USA, well-trafficked websites offer galleries of tens of thousands of racy amateur self-portraits surreptitiously downloaded from women's private MySpace or Facebook accounts or maliciously provided by ex-boyfriends. It's not just celebrities who share intimate imagery.

A Primal Means of Communicating

Though men are so eager to gaze upon women's candid photos they're willing to risk jail time by hacking cellphones, pictures of men's private parts usually come to public attention when a recipient is offended; German Olympian Ariane Friedrich, for example, outed a man on Facebook for sending her a photograph of his manhood. These pickle shots tend to elicit protests and consternation. Men do not question why Scarlett Johansson or Jessica Alba might want to sext bare skin to a guy. But women everywhere ask, 'What are men thinking when they send us photos of their junk?' The answer is that men may not be thinking at all; they may be compelled by an unconscious, evolutionary urge inherited from our primate ancestors.

Male monkeys and apes routinely display their penises to females to indicate sexual interest. Primatologist Frans de Waal writes in *Peacemaking Among Primates*: "Since bonobos can sheath their penis, nothing is visible most of the time. When the organ does appear, however, it is not only impressive in size, but its bright pink color makes it stand out against the dark fur. Males invite others by presenting with legs wide apart and back arched, often flicking the penis up and down—a powerful signal."

Joe Francis (front), with his Girls Gone Wild videos, has tapped into young women's willingness to exhibit themselves for a T-shirt and the opportunity to be ogled by millions of men, the author says.

Men do not share women's desire to be desired. Instead, they emulate their bonobo brethren: The internet is saturated with penis self-portraits from every nation on Earth. At any given moment, one in four cameras on the webcam network ChatRoulette are aimed at a penis. On the adult networking site Fantasti.cc, 36 percent of men use an image of a penis as their avatar; only 5 percent of women use a vagina. On Reddit's heterosexual Gone Wild forum in 2010, where users were free to post uncensored pictures of themselves, 35 percent of images self-posted by men consisted of penises.

Though hordes of men pay to peruse amateur photography depicting the anatomy of ladies, not a single website collects cash from ladies interested in surveying amateur photography of phalluses.

Anyone who has seen a koteka, the elaborate two-foot-long penis cap worn by men in Papua New Guinea, can easily believe that men have inherited our hominid cousins' exhibitionist urge regarding the penis. In fact, male exhibitionism has long been understood by clinical psychologists as a non-dangerous compulsion: Men who flash their organ to strangers rarely seek contact afterward, instead describing a powerful sense of relief from the display alone. Of course, the yawn is also a powerful biological compulsion, but as we learned in grade school it's always preferable to cover your mouth.

EIGHT

Sexting Results from Normal Teen Sexual Expression

Tracy Clark-Flory

> The urge to sext racy photos of oneself is part of normal teen sexual exploration, argues Tracy Clark-Flory in the following viewpoint. Clark-Flory reminisces about her own teen years, which she says were filled with sexual but safe experimentation, which included taking nude pictures of herself and sharing them with her boyfriend. Sexting is the same thing, she says, and chides legislators who want to make such behavior illegal or criminally punishable. Sexting is how young people experiment with their bodies, their image, and how others perceive them, and Clark-Flory says they deserve a certain amount of freedom to do this. She concludes that sexting is most often part of a teen's normal sexual development and any policies addressing it should be crafted around this premise.
>
> Clark-Flory is a staff writer at *Salon*, an online newsmagazine that features commentary on a wide range of issues.

I just recently performed an archaeological dig on my childhood closet, which has been perfectly preserved in the state it was in when I flew the nest. Amid all the empty bottles of Smirnoff Ice and aimlessly doodled-on binders, I found a stockpile of what might be referred to in court as "child pornography"—but it was self-made with my high school boyfriend. The first thought I had when I saw the images—black-and-white printouts from a webcam—was how sweet the shots were, despite being mildly explicit. Here were two teenagers safely and lovingly exploring their bodies and sexualities—and because the images were kept strictly for our eyes only, they maintained that innocence.

Sexy Pics Are Normal

That's why I'm encouraged by news that late yesterday [March 14, 2011,] New Jersey approved a bill that would allow teenagers caught "sexting" to avoid being prosecuted as child pornographers. The bill is based on the wacky notion that teens shouldn't be labeled as sex offenders for the rest of their lives for taking dirty self-portraits, or possessing X-rated photos of their sweetheart who, in many cases, they are legally allowed to have sex with.

New Jersey assemblyman Jon Bramnick believes that teens should not be prosecuted for sexting.

(Although, that was not the case for me, as the age of consent in California is 18. Whoops.) This measure is a great step toward a saner adult attitude toward teen sexuality, and other states should look to it as a blueprint. But there's also room for improvement.

The bill gives teens the option of paying for an educational program as a way to avoid a damaging criminal record. Assemblyman Jon Bramnick told NBC that the measure "sends a clear signal to the Judiciary that when young people make a mistake, this Legislature is saying, 'give them a chance, give them an option other than a criminal past.'" He's absolutely right—it is absurd for "sexting" to land a teen on the sex offender registry—but Bramnick, and the measure itself, would be *more* right if they allowed that sometimes it isn't a mistake or wrong when teenagers take sexy self-snapshots, that it can be part of normal sexual development.

Teens Need Some Freedom to Experiment

Now, to be clear, I don't think it's a good idea for teenagers to distribute naked photos of themselves. More often than not it's a bad idea to digitally share naked pics, even with a committed lover, and we should communicate that to teens. (We should also be educating kids, and adults, about the profound potential for embarrassment and professional consequences in digitally sharing even personal images that are not pornographic.) If we were really concerned with the well-being and personal rights of teenagers, though, we would create a legislative safe space for sexual exploration.

Clearly, the major concern is that by allowing teens to even take or possess naked self-portraits, we would be sanctioning the production of child pornography. It's true that once an image is digitalized its reach can be enormous—whether it's on a hackable computer or spread through a chain of text messages. But we should find a way to both protect teens against exploitation and allow them a reasonable degree of sexual autonomy. Save the prosecutions and the example-making for those who disseminate pornographic images of minors other than themselves (and that would include, say, the girlfriend who texts an image of

Reasons Young People Sext

Getting attention, making a boyfriend or girlfriend happy, and to be flirtatious are all reasons given for sexting by teens who do it.

Question: *What are the reasons that you have sent/posted suggestive messages or nude/seminude pictures/videos (of yourself)?* *

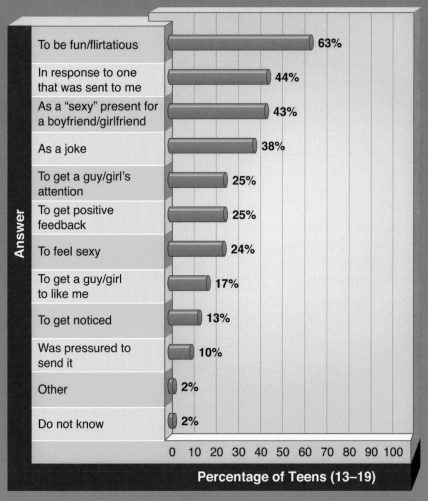

*Answers exceed 100% because respondents were allowed to select more than one answer.

Taken from: National Campaign to Prevent Teen and Unplanned Pregnancy. *Sex and Tech: Results from a Survey of Teens and Young Adults*, 2008, p. 12.

her ex-boyfriend's penis to the entire school in an act of retaliation). There certainly are no easy black-and-white answers here, especially when it comes to the blunt instrument of the law, but we should keep striving for smarter legislation—and the New Jersey bill is a start.

A Normal Rite of Passage

As for my recent discovery in my childhood closet? I threw all the photos away, impulsively and in a moment of fear. I mean, child pornography, *eek*! A big part of me regrets it, though. I don't see any good reason why it should be illegal for me to possess those images. And it would have been nice to dig the photos out of a safe hiding place when I have high school kids of my own and to remember what it was like to be a lusty teenager in love.

NINE

America's Sex-Crazed Culture Promotes Sexting

Leah Hird

In the following viewpoint Leah Hird argues that
America's sex-obsessed culture encourages teens to text
racy or nude photos of themselves to others. Hird points
out that many of the celebrities whom teen girls admire
have either been photographed in sexy or provocative
outfits or acted in movies that portray women as sex
objects. Likewise, many of the television shows intended
for teen audiences show girls in skimpy outfits, or leveraging their sexuality for popularity or social acceptance.
It is no wonder, then, according to Hird, that teen girls
think the best way to get attention, be popular, or otherwise feel valued is to sext degrading pictures of themselves. Hird concludes that America's teen girls need to
be told that sexually humiliating oneself is unacceptable,
inappropriate, and a terrible way to get positive, con-
structive attention.

At the time this article was originally published, Hird
was an intern for Concerned Women for America, a
conservative women's organization that supports policies, laws, and movements that are in accordance with
biblical principles.

Sex texting is the newest trend among middle and high school students. Similar to text messaging, sex texting, or "sexting" as it is more commonly called, is the practice of taking nude pictures of bodies and body parts and electronically sending [them] to another person. Typically, a boyfriend is the intended receiver as girls try to impress or win the young man's affection, but often after a bad break up, the ex-lover will forward the obscene photos to friends who forward it to their friends and so forth. Students are even uploading this material to networks like MySpace where their friends can have easy access to them.

Many parents, school administrators, and investigators are concerned, even frightened, noting that photos like these could easily get into the hands of the wrong people—pedophiles and sexual predators. Moreover, parents are concerned that their teens will encounter child pornography charges since it is illegal for children under 18 to produce, receive, or distribute sexually explicit photos on their cell phones. Even more upsetting for many is the fact that most teens are either unaware of the danger, or shrug it off as ordinary behavior.

Born of a Sex-Obsessed Culture

Forgive me, but I have to ask, should any of us be surprised? In a society fixated on sex and sex appeal, is it any wonder that "sexting" has become popular in middle schools and high schools? After all, these girls—the disproportionate source of the photos—are only mimicking what they see their celebrity role models doing.

Think about it—Miley Cyrus, [Britney] Spears, Christina Aguilera, Vanessa Hudgens, Lindsay Lohan, Paris Hilton, Beyoncé Knowles, Jessica Alba, and Keira Knightly—all of these celebrities have either participated in provocative photo shoots scantily clad or completely nude, or have filmed "steamy" sex scenes which have marked the height of their careers. Moreover, they have been rewarded for their behavior, gaining fortune and popularity—even if it's popularity for doing wrong as is the case with Cyrus, Spears, and Hudgens.

These varied images of sexuality in US culture are displayed at the Museum of Sex. Many adults think that America's sex-obsessed culture encourages teens to sext.

Sex Is Glorified and Exalted

As Sharlene Azam from *Prism* magazine (September/October 2008) explains, "Bombarded with images that link a woman's value to her sexual willingness, girls see their role models engaging in graphic, exhibitionist behavior—and being rewarded for it. . . . Anyone who has ever stood in a supermarket checkout line knows that . . . today's female pop icons are sex objects to be alternately exalted, ogled, emulated, critiqued, condemned, pitied, and recycled . . . *ad nauseum*."

Even teen-targeted television shows like *Gossip Girl* and *One Tree Hill*, magazines like *Seventeen* and *CosmoGirl*, countless underwear and body wash commercials, and teen fashions glorify sexiness and tell teens to do likewise. Movies, too, not only tell teens that obsession with sexuality is good but that pornography itself is no big deal.

Sexting by Gender

Boys are more likely to send and receive naked or semi-naked pictures than are girls.

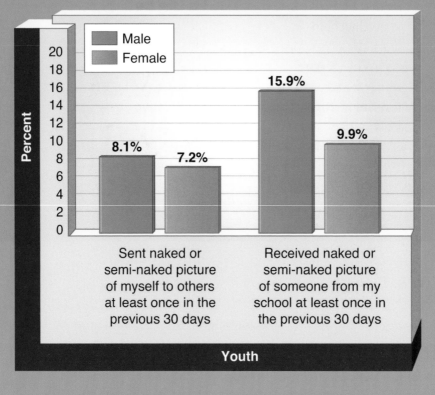

Taken from: Sameer Hinduja and Justin Patchin. "Sexting: A Brief Guide for Educators." Cyberbullying Research Center, 2010, p. 2.

In the recent R-rated film, *Zack and Miri Make a Porno*, two financially struggling best friends and roommates decide to earn a living by making a porn movie. Audiences are supposed to find the movie humorous and accept the pat message that "sex isn't sexy without love, commitment, and fidelity," as *Entertainment Weekly*'s Lisa Schwarzbaum comments in a film review. Thankfully, the movie was not a box office hit, but am I the only one utterly disgusted that a movie mocking and downplaying pornography—a known factor in rape, sex trafficking, and pedophilia crimes—would even be at the theatres?

Mixed Messages Hurt Children

Clearly, our culture is sending teens mixed messages, telling them it is wrong to produce and distribute sexually explicit pictures, but that it is okay to be entertained by those who essentially do the same thing. This has to end.

As Dr. Janice Shaw Crouse, Director and Senior Fellow of Concerned Women for America's Beverly LaHaye Institute, notes, "Too many people shrug their shoulders and turn away as though offensive material and behavior are not their business. People are not outraged; instead, they accept images on their television screens and computer monitors that would have shocked previous generations and should shock ours."

You and I are part of the culture that sends teens mixed messages. That is why we must give them an unambiguous message and reject sexual obscenity not only on their cell phones but also in movies, television shows, magazines, fashion trends, and even video games. Contact the clothing stores that profit from sexualizing teens. Be strict on the entertainment your teens are viewing. Hollywood and the other industries that obsess over sex understand only one thing—money. We have got to hit them where it hurts. Let us lead the way in giving teens a clear message: sexual obscenity is wrong no matter how it is packaged.

TEN

Sexting Is a Valid Form of Self-Expression for Teens

Amy Adele Hasinoff

In the following viewpoint Amy Adele Hasinoff argues that teens have the right to sext. She is glad that certain courts have found teens who distributed sexual images of themselves not guilty of child pornography, but she says these cases did not go far enough. Not only are such teens innocent of child pornography, she says, but they have a right to take and distribute such images under the First Amendment. In Hasinoff's opinion, the right to free speech includes being able to take pictures of themselves and distribute to whomever they want. Hasinoff says that hysteria over teen sexting misses the fact that such pictures are taken in a safe and consensual way. Furthermore, they do not put teens at risk for sexually transmitted disease or pregnancy, and thus should be celebrated as a safe, harmless form of sexual expression. Hasinoff concludes that no court, law, or policy should violate teens' right to sext.

Hasinoff is a doctoral fellow at the Institute of Communications Research at the University of Illinois, Urbana-Champaign. Her doctoral dissertation critically examines teenage girls' sexual self-expression, including sexting.

In early 2009, parents of nearly twenty students at a high school in Tunkhannock, Pennsylvania received a letter from district attorney George Skumanick explaining that school officials had found sexually explicit photos of classmates on some of the students' cell phones. The students appearing in or possessing the photos could face child pornography charges unless they agreed to complete an education program and serve six months of probation, including random drug testing.

Ignoring Teens' Right to Sext

Most of the students agreed to a version of Skumanick's deal, while Marissa Miller, two other students, and their parents, sought the help of the Pennsylvania American Civil Liberties Union [ACLU]. In March 2009, they obtained a restraining order preventing the prosecutor from filing child pornography charges, and in March of 2010, a federal appeals court upheld the decision.

This case did not address the girls' right to freedom of expression, but instead succeeded on the fact that forcing the girls to attend Skumanick's education program would violate two constitutional rights: (1) the parents' right to control the upbringing of their children and (2) the girls' right to freedom from compelled speech. This strategy was indeed successful, but the case sets a disturbing precedent keeping adolescents' right to freedom of expression off the table. Since this crucial issue is rarely debated in discussions about sexting, I argue that we need seriously to consider adolescents' right to sext.

It Is Wrong to Avoid the Real Issue

Child pornography laws make no exception for minors under 18 years old who create sexually explicit images of themselves. In a state like Illinois, where the age of consent is 17, two 17-year-olds can legally have sex with each other, but if they create a digital image of their sex acts, even for their own use, this depiction is technically child pornography. The ACLU can't defend the girls' First Amendment rights to sext without fundamentally challenging the constitutionality of child pornography laws.

Witold J. Walczak, left, director of the ACLU of Pennsylvania, and Mary Joe Miller challenged the child pornography charges filed against Miller's daughter for sexting.

Instead, the ACLU disputes the prosecutor's claim that the photos qualify as child pornography, arguing that the images were not sexual and do not, as Pennsylvania law specifies, depict "nudity if such nudity is depicted for the purpose of sexual stimulation or gratification of any person who might view such depiction." In their press release, the ACLU describes the images: "One [photograph] shows Marissa Miller and Grace Kelly from the waist up wearing white bras. The other depicts Nancy Doe (a pseudonym) . . . standing outside a shower with a bath towel wrapped around her body beneath her breasts."

In their argument before the federal appeals court, the ACLU maintains that the topless photo of one of the girls is "an innocent artistic image of a minor in a state of simple partial nudity, not a sexually provocative image intended to titillate." A legal analyst explains that the appeal court's final decision in favor of the girls both relies on the assumption that "any prosecution on child-porn-related charges would be invalid [and] . . . simultaneously disavows any [explicit] position on that question."

By avoiding this discussion, the court avoids considering if child pornography laws, first drafted in the late 1970s well before the ease and availability of digital image production and distribution technologies, might pose an overbroad and unconstitutional limitation on young people's first amendment rights.

Teens Have the Right to Self-Expression

Instead of arguing that minors deserve the right to freedom of expression, the ACLU's press releases and public statements suggest that sexting teens should not be prosecuted because they are too immature to be held accountable for their actions. Many of their public comments about the case assert that teens are immature and foolish, which mobilizes public sympathies, but puts the ACLU in the strange position of seeking to protect some of teens' legal rights while simultaneously affirming that teens are not worthy of the same legal rights as adults. In a CNN interview, anchor Mike Galanos asks lead ACLU attorney in the Miller case, Witold Walczak: "You're not saying—I want to be clear about this—that kids have the right to sext," to which Walczak replies that he agrees "absolutely" that teens do not have the "right to sext." Galanos continues: "It's good to send them the message: it's not right, girls, you're laying the groundwork for something that could be worse down the road."

The ACLU press release, which was widely used in newspaper articles about the case, quotes Walczak: "These are just kids being irresponsible and careless; they are not criminals and they certainly haven't committed child pornography." A *Wired* article quotes Walczak: "Teens are stupid and impulsive and clueless. . . . But that doesn't make them criminals." Attempting to garner sympathy for young sexters, Walczak insists with these statements that because teenagers are "careless, clueless, stupid, and impulsive," they should not be held legally accountable for their

How Does Receiving a Sext Make Teens Feel?

A group of thirteen- to nineteen-year-olds reported feeling mostly positive emotions upon receiving a sext.

Question: Thinking about suggestive messages or nude/ seminude pictures/videos that you ever received, how did getting them make you feel?*

Answer	Percentage of Teens (13–19)
Surprised	55%
Amused	54%
Turned on	53%
Excited	44%
Happy	40%
More interested in hooking up with sender	27%
Creeped out	22%
Most interested in dating sender	22%
Grossed out	15%
Turned off	15%
Embarrassed	14%
Less interested in hooking up with sender	14%
Less interested in dating sender	13%
Included	12%
Disappointed	7%
Angry	6%
Scared	4%
Other	4%

*Answers exceed 100% because respondents could select multiple answers.

Taken from: National Campaign to Prevent Teen and Unplanned Pregnancy. *Sex and Tech: Results from a Survey of Teens and Young Adults*, 2008.

actions, arguing that adolescents have no criminal intent and barely have the ability to judge their own actions.

Society Should Celebrate Safe Sexual Acts Like Sexting

Since at least 15 states are in the process of writing new sexting legislation, it is crucial to examine how we make sense of sexting. I argue that it is counter-productive to understand sexting as "innocent and nonsexual" or as the result of "impulsiveness and carelessness." Instead, we should look at sexting as an opportunity to redefine our skewed perceptions of teen girls' sexuality and to reconsider our inconsistent child pornography and age of consent laws.

While sometimes images are distributed among teenagers without the permission of the person depicted, laws do not currently distinguish this unacceptable behavior from consensual sexting. Rather than criminalizing adolescent sexual self-expression, we need to create new legal and educational policies that acknowledge and celebrate safe, consensual teenage sex acts, and demand that teens should have the right to sext.

ELEVEN

Sexting Is Not a Valid Form of Self-Expression for Teens

L. Brent Bozell III

It is always inappropriate for teens to take and text nude pictures of themselves, argues L. Brent Bozell III in the following viewpoint. He discusses how teens who have been caught sexting have defended their behavior by invoking their constitutional right to free speech. Bozell is appalled that some adults would accept this defense, saying that sexting has serious consequences and can forever ruin a young person's life. Bozell thinks that sexting may be appropriate for adults, but never for teens, who remain very vulnerable to sexting's real and dreadful consequences. He laments that today's adults would care so little for teens so as not to try to protect them from sexting. Bozell concludes that sexting is not a valid form of expression for teens and is deeply disappointed in anyone who says otherwise.

Bozell is a syndicated columnist whose articles appear in numerous conservative publications.

Can a child be accused of child pornography? Could a child then be formally charged and convicted of it? These are the questions raised by the disturbing new trend called "sexting," teenagers sending nude or semi-nude pictures around on their cell phones. In some jurisdictions, prosecutors are playing hardball, threatening that students caught with naughty pictures could face jail time and being registered as sex offenders. At a minimum, prosecutors are demanding a 10-hour rehab program.

Does this offense seem too casual to justify throwing the legal book at children? Consider that it's undeniable that if Johnny was a day or two over 18 and was sending around these images, he'd be treated as a sicko—with prison time a real possibility.

Do We Have No Shame?

In our litigious culture, it was only a matter of time: Now the "sexting" perpetrators are fighting back. In Wyoming County, Pennsylvania, three female students and their parents hired the American Civil Liberties Union to sue the county prosecutor for daring to suggest something wrong was done and insisting a ten-hour "re-education" program was necessary.

It's a thorny issue, to be sure. When legislators passed child-pornography laws, who could have imagined our culture would grow so decadent that children would be distributing nude pictures of themselves to other children? Who also would have predicted that some parents would be unashamed enough of their children's behavior to hire the ACLU and sue authorities for enforcing child-porn laws?

"Prosecutors should not be using a nuclear-weapon-type charge like child pornography against kids who have no criminal intent and are merely doing stupid things," proclaimed the ACLU lawyer, Witold Walczak.

But this is something that just cannot be dismissed as kids "doing stupid things.

Sexting Is Serious, Even Deadly

"Sexting" has quickly grown from rare to commonplace. A survey of 1,280 teenagers and young adults released in December [2008] by the National Campaign to Prevent Teenage and Unplanned Pregnancy and CosmoGirl.com found that 20 percent of teenagers

What Teens Think of People Who Sext

When asked their opinion of those who sext, many teens reported a wide array of impressions.

Taken from: National Campaign to Prevent Teen and Unplanned Pregnancy. *Sex and Tech: Results from a Survey of Teens and Young Adults*, 2008.

*Question: How much do you agree or disagree that each of the following describes the **activity** of sending suggestive messages or nude/seminude pictures/video of oneself?**

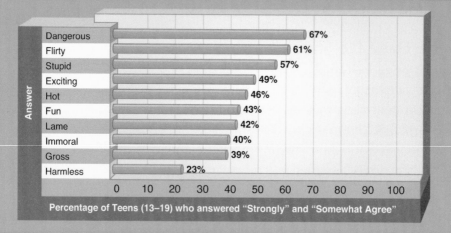

Answer	Percentage
Dangerous	67%
Flirty	61%
Stupid	57%
Exciting	49%
Hot	46%
Fun	43%
Lame	42%
Immoral	40%
Gross	39%
Harmless	23%

Percentage of Teens (13–19) who answered "Strongly" and "Somewhat Agree"

*Question: How much do you agree or disagree that each of the following describes the **people** who send suggestive messages or nude/seminude pictures/video of themselves?**

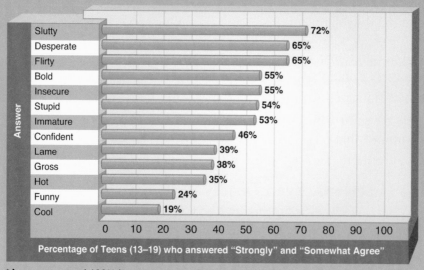

Answer	Percentage
Slutty	72%
Desperate	65%
Flirty	65%
Bold	55%
Insecure	55%
Stupid	54%
Immature	53%
Confident	46%
Lame	39%
Gross	38%
Hot	35%
Funny	24%
Cool	19%

Percentage of Teens (13–19) who answered "Strongly" and "Somewhat Agree"

*Answers exceed 100% because respondents were allowed to select multiple answers.

and 33 percent of young adults ages 20 to 26 said they had sent or posted nude or semi-nude photos of themselves.

The numbers were higher for the number who would admit they've received nude or semi-nude images: 31 percent of teens and 46 percent of young adults. They know it rarely stays private: 72 percent of teens and 68 percent of young adults agreed that sexy pictures often end up being "seen by more than the intended recipients."

When the subject of a "sexting" is famous, the image often ends up on the Internet. A nude photo of Vanessa Hudgens, the teenaged female star of Disney's "High School Musical" movies, went from private e-mail to Internet sensation.

It can even end in suicide. *People* magazine reported that last year, Jessie Logan, a senior at a Cincinnati [Ohio]–area high school, took a nude photo of herself and sent it to a boy she was dating. She then learned the photo was being distributed at four area high schools. Other students began taunting her as a "whore." She hanged herself.

Teens Are Not Adults

People's article on "sexting" cited the case of two 14-year-old boys in Massachusetts who received a photo of a 13-year-old girl exposing a breast. Parents were shocked that authorities were weighing child-pornography charges. Said one father: "What they did was wrong, but did they know it was wrong? . . . These are 14-year-old kids with 14-year-old minds, not adults."

Once parents get over the idea of seventh-grade girls flashing their private parts for the camera, it's clear that teenagers are not identical to adults who would prey on a 13-year-old. It's shocking to imagine ending up on the wrong side of the law by merely receiving an unsolicited pornographic image. Authorities aren't convicting children, but using the law as a teaching tool and trying to put a stop to a toxic new trend.

Those Who Defend Sexting Are Wrong

It's obvious that some experts will be quoted to defend it. The *Pittsburgh* [Pennsylvania] *Post-Gazette* found Texas A&M

professor Christopher Ferguson, who called the trend unwise, but "We would have done it, too, if we would have had the cool phones. We didn't do it because we didn't have the technology."

The same goes for defense attorneys. Public defender Dante Bertani protested a case of "sexting" teenagers in Greensburg,

Conservative columnist Brent Bozell III believes that teens and children should not be able to use the Constitution's right of free speech to justify sexting.

Pennsylvania: "Law enforcement gets carried away with what they believe is their duty to find everyone who spits on the sidewalk guilty of murder."

Bertani must not have heard of the Cincinnati suicide. He failed to acknowledge that spit on the sidewalk evaporates, but pornographic images can hang around forever on the "cool phones" and the Internet. Prosecutors and parents alike are correct to put the brakes on this mistake wherever it's discovered.

The civil libertarians may wish to reconsider their position. They claim it's a private matter best resolved by parental responsibility. Would it follow that their parental irresponsibility should make the parent the legally liable party?

TWELVE

Sexting Should Be a Crime

Mike Todd

Mike Todd is the assistant prosecuting attorney for Summit County, Ohio. In the following viewpoint he presents testimony to the Ohio House of Representatives on the need to make sexting a crime. Todd warns that sexting is a widespread problem with serious consequences. Teens need to be dissuaded from taking nude photos of themselves and sending them to others, and making the act a crime is the best way to do this, he says. Adults should not worry that criminal punishments will be handed out unnecessarily—Todd says that all of the punishments his county has doled out for sexting have been appropriate, measured, and reasonable. Todd says very harsh punishments for sexting must be kept on the table, though: Teens will be less likely to sext if they know the possibility of criminal punishment exists. Todd concludes it would be a mistake to decriminalize sexting and urges lawmakers to make sexting a crime punishable with severe consequences.

My name is Mike Todd and I am an Assistant Prosecuting Attorney for Summit County. I am here with Julie Bruns, Assistant Prosecuting Attorney for Montgomery County. We appreciate the opportunity to present opponent testimony for

Michael D. Todd, "Opponent Testimony on House Bill 53," Ohio House of Representatives, March 16, 2011.

House Bill 53, legislation to clarify Ohio's "sexting" laws. While we applaud the State Legislature's effort to protect our State's youths from this dangerous trend, we have reservations to portions of House Bill 53 that we believe need to be addressed.

Sexting Is a Widespread Problem

Over the last two years, the Summit County Prosecutor's Office (SCPO) has been in contact with over 12,000 junior high and high school students throughout Summit County as part of an educational outreach program. Our outreach program has been aimed at informing juveniles of both the legal and life consequences of sexting. As part of our presentation we focused on the potential of having to register as a sex offender and outlined the possibility of a felony level conviction for egregious conduct.

Another element of our outreach program was the gathering of anonymous information from students about their attitudes on sexting. We wanted to gauge whether or not our presentation had an impact on their thought process. A shocking 13% of middle school and 41% of high school students stated that they had received a nude or partially nude photo by text or internet

I THOUGHT IT WAS THE LAW THAT WAS TRYING TO KEEP UP WITH TECHNOLOGY...

WWW.MILTPRIGGEE.COM

SNAP CLICK

NEWS ITEM: STILL NO LAWS ADDRESSING TEENAGE PHENOMENA OF SEXTING.

prior to our presentation. The vast majority of these students (80.7%) stated they recognized the person in the photo. After the presentations, 85% of the students stated, that now knowing the consequences, they would not engage in sexting.

Harsh Punishments Rarely Handed Out

Many critics of current laws applied to sexting have stated that these laws are "draconian" and that the punishment for sexting far outweighs the conduct. However, we feel it important to note that the current statutes do in fact provide an adequate array of charges for a prosecutor to exercise discretion to ensure that the conduct fits the crime. Summit County conducted a brief survey

After participating in an Ohio outreach and educational program on the criminal consequences of sexting, 85 percent of the teen participants stated that they would not engage in sexting.

of County Prosecutors' Offices throughout the State to see how they were actually handling sexting cases. Of the fifteen counties that responded there was a total of 177 sexting case. Only 58 of these cases resulted in formal charges, while the other cases went through diversion programs set up by County Prosecutors' Offices. Of these 58 cases, only 6 cases were resolved at the felony level, and not one of these offenders was required to register as a sex offender. . . .

Criminal Consequences Help Dissuade Teens

Most teens we deal with know that engaging in sexting is morally wrong, but very few understand the long term consequences of their actions. Being able to tell them there are very serious consequences *does* have an impact on them. To date, not one person who participated in the MCPO [Montgomery County Prosecutor's Office] juvenile sexting diversion has re-offended.

Having spoken personally with many of these children, it is clear that the stiffer the *potential* consequences the more likely they were to view sexting as a serious offense with serious consequences and not engage in the conduct. Decriminalizing sexting and similar actions sends the wrong message to the wrong population for the wrong reason. Ohio County and Juvenile Prosecutors intend to protect the victims of sexting and use their discretion to *appropriately* prosecute offenders. . . .

In Kids' Best Interest

We know that the field of sexting legislation is uncharted territory in the State of Ohio and that the decisions this honorable committee have to make are not easy. We ask you to consider to what ends are we establishing laws criminalizing sexting. We feel it is to protect the victims of sexting and to help educate and prevent juveniles from engaging in this dangerous practice.

THIRTEEN

Sexting Should Not Be a Crime

Sonya Ziaja

Sexting should not be treated as a crime, argues Sonya Ziaja in the following viewpoint. She says that adults and lawmakers are in a hurry to address teen sexting, and as a result they have rushed to impose criminal consequences without fully understanding the problem. Ziaja says that, in the process, they have overlooked several critical facts about sexting, one of which is that it may not be a huge problem. Not that many teens do it, and it is extremely rare that something terrible results from it, says Ziaja. Therefore, it is unnecessary and inappropriate to assign criminal consequences to sexting. In many cases, says Ziaja, the criminal consequences wreak more havoc on a teen's life than does the act of sexting. Ziaja says sexting would be better addressed with outreach and educational programs that treat sexting cases more like a social problem rather than a crime.

Ziaja owns Ziaja Consulting and writes regularly for *Legal Match's Law Blog* and other online sites, such as AlterNet.

The *New York Times* recently reported that several states are considering bills that tackle juvenile sexting (the transmission of nude or "provocative" pictures to another person, usually by cell phone). Lawmakers are trying to address sexting largely because of a serious loophole in federal and state child pornography laws. In most states, when a teen sends a nude or "provocative" image of him/herself to another teen, it is not legally distinct from producing, distributing, or possessing child pornography. Clearly child pornography laws are meant to protect children from exploitation. The penalties for distributing sexually explicit images of minors include lengthy prison sentences and a lifetime of being a registered sex offender. These penalties, however, make little sense if the victim and the perpetrator are the same person.

Criminalizing Sexting Without Understanding It

All of the state bills consider lighter penalties than currently exist for juvenile sexting. Many include provisions that redirect teens who are caught sexting to education programs, in order to avoid criminal prosecution. The bills use a variety of approaches to address sexting among teens and tweens. But one thing remains consistent in all of them. Each bill retains the possibility of criminal prosecution for sexting.

It is important to differentiate teen sexting from child pornography. But by specifically defining sexting as a criminal activity, state legislatures are rushing to stop a form of sexual expression without first trying to understand it. Why aren't we having a broader conversation about what the most appropriate response is to teen sexting?

Sexting May Not Even Be a Big Problem

Legislators claim that sexting is a widespread phenomenon among youth, that it endangers teens, and that prosecution of youth for child pornography is too harsh. While these reasons may indicate a need for swift action, it's important to examine each of them first.

Data are inconsistent on exactly how prevalent sexting is among teens and tweens, and varies depending on the definition of sexting, and the age range sampled. A survey published by the Pew Center in late 2009 suggests that about 15 percent of teens receive sext-messages or nude images of people they know, while only about 4 percent send these messages. The Pew Center defined sexting as sending sexually explicit images, and sampled minors age 12 to 17. Another, often cited, survey was published by the National Campaign to Prevent Teen and Unplanned Pregnancy and CosmoGirl.com in 2008. That survey used different criteria and concluded that about 20 percent of teens have sent a sext message. However, it used a broader definition of sexting that included sexually suggestive written messages as well as risqué images. It also used information from an older age range (13 to 19) than the Pew Center used. The CosmoGirl.com results are also questionable because they included only teens who voluntarily responded to an online survey, thereby ensuring a skewed sample. Because it was an online survey, it is likely that the survey overrepresented tech-savvy teens and teens interested in sexting. Indeed, even the press release for the survey states that "Respondents do not constitute a probability sample."

The surveys are nonetheless in agreement on certain findings. A small minority of teens have sent a sext message. More teens receive messages than send them. And, older teens are more likely to send sexually suggestive messages (i.e., as they mature sexually, they are more likely to engage in sexting). The data do not suggest, however, that there is a looming sexting crisis sufficient to necessitate immediate action without further investigation of the matter.

Bad Sexting Consequences Are Rare and Extreme

Even if it is only a small number of teens who engage in sexting, perhaps the quick and nearly unanimous response of lawmakers can be explained by the severity of the consequences of sexting. There is certainly a dark side to teen sexting. Two particularly well-publicized examples are the tragic suicide of Jessica Logan, an

The mother of a girl who committed suicide after her sext was made public testifies before a legislative committee. The viewpoint author argues that such cases are rare and should not generate harsh penalties for sexting.

eighteen-year-old Ohio woman, and the prosecution and subsequent conviction of Philip Albert, a Florida teen, for distributing child pornography.

Jessica Logan's case began in high school when she sent a nude image of herself to her then-boyfriend. After their relationship ended, her ex forwarded the image to several girls at the school. The girls, and later other classmates, harassed Jessica both at school and online, branding her as a "slut" and a "whore." Jessica sought assistance from the school and from the police, but no one seemed to help. Eventually, Jessica ended her life. A subsequent court case was brought by her parents against the school for failing to help her and prevent her suicide.

Philip Albert received photos taken by his 16-year-old girl-friend of her naked body. When the relationship ended bitterly, Philip, consumed by teenage angst and anger, forwarded the photos of his ex to her family, teachers, and friends. At the age of 18, he was then arrested for distributing child pornography. He was convicted, sentenced to five years' probation, and is now registered as a sex offender until he is 43 years old.

Jessica's turmoil points to the potential emotional problems that can arise from sexting, while Philip's situation demonstrates possible negative consequences of prosecution from sexting, if the laws are not updated. Both of these outcomes should be preventable. To do justice to either of these victims, however, takes careful consideration of the sexting issue.

Moreover, these cases are not the norm. It is extremely rare for teens involved in sexting to commit suicide over sexting-relating conflicts. And as the Logan family's court case demonstrates, perhaps the real issue was the lack of resources around bullying, rather than Jessica's initial sext message. Nancy Wilard, of The Center for Safe and Responsible Internet Use, concludes similarly, that sexting itself is not the danger, "[the few sexting-related suicides] have taken place where there was massive adult overreaction, which legitimized peer harassment, and then abject failure of the adults to stop the harassment."

The Overzealous Rush to Criminalize

There are also very few sexting cases that end in successful prosecution for distribution of child pornography. Although the current law in many states allows for it, prosecutorial discretion combined with the absurdly high penalties of conviction has meant

Sexting Laws in the United States

Most states do not yet have laws that specifically address sexting, so minors can be charged with child pornography or be registered as a sex offender. Other states are considering or have passed laws that distinguish between minors and adults, so as to offer less harsh sentences to teens who sext.

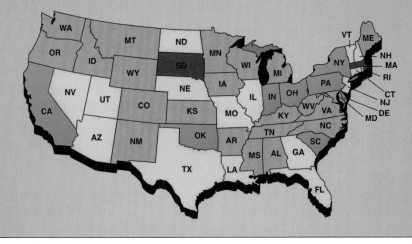

■ Sexting-specific legislation failed to become law—law does not distinguish between minors and adults.

■ No specific statute for sexting, but law allows anyone, regardless of age, to be prosecuted for possessing or distributing sexually explicit pictures of minors.

□ Has a specific law to address sexting, or distinguishes between minors and adults in some way.

■ Sexting-specific legislation has been proposed or is pending.

Taken from: Mobile Media Guard.com. "U.S. Sexting Laws and Regulations." Parental Solutions, 2011.

that most prosecutors have not followed that route. In Texas, for example, no minor has ever been prosecuted for sexting despite the fact that state law allows for such prosecution and teenagers across the state do send texts. In other states, a few overzealous prosecutors have used the loophole in the laws to prosecute teens as sex offenders. The idea of unchecked prosecutors is certainly disconcerting, but moving forward, diversionary programs and lighter sentences may actually mean more prosecution overall for teen sexting.

It seems clear that the argument that the costs of sexting demand immediate legislation, without significant deliberation, do not hold up to scrutiny.

The fact that the legislative push to criminalize kids for sexting has not been accompanied by a sober scientific inquiry about teen sexuality may have more to do with the adults who make the laws than the teens at whom the laws are aimed. Adults are often uncomfortable with adolescent sexuality and as such attempt to penalize the expression of it. As Professor Thomas Hubbard writes in the *Journal of Boyhood Studies*, it is not uncommon in our culture for adults to fetishize the "purity" of youth. One aspect of fetishizing imagined youthful purity is that adults lash out at youth who display or act on their sexuality.

It may also simply be politically unfeasible for legislators to take a reasoned approach or to question what is normal behavior when it comes to teens and sex. In her article on sexting, Susie Wilson points to her failed attempts to persuade one New Jersey legislator to vote against a bill that required teachers to "stress abstinence" in sex education. The lawmaker explained that to vote against the bill would be to sacrifice his career over the issue, something he was not willing to do. In short, being realistic about teen sexuality can be contentious.

Alternatives Should Be Pursued

The movement to criminalize sexting cannot be blamed on a lack of alternatives. There have been a few notable outliers when it comes to the push to criminalize teen sexting.

The Indiana State Senate is one of these. In 2009, it drafted a resolution that called on the legislative council to create a Sentencing Policy Study Committee "to ensure that [Indiana's] criminal justice system remains fair and equitable." The Committee would take into account "the psychology of sexuality and sexual development[,] the psychology of sexual deviants and deviance[,] and the mental development of children and young adults and how this affects the ability to make certain judgments." Likewise, the state of South Dakota decided to table its sexting bill, instead of hastily pushing it through.

Another example of restraint comes from the Australian Psychological Society [APS] Ltd's Submission to the Joint Select Committee on Cyber-Safety. The APS considers sexting as a form of cyber-bullying, and makes several recommendations for youth, families, schools and lawmakers. Its prescription focuses on wide-spread education, and does not at all encourage criminal penalties, nor the threat of criminal penalties. Specifically, it suggests that the risks of sexting should be communicated accurately and that we should "avoid over-emphasizing the risks." Education for youth should support the development of critical thinking "that invites [youth] to question attitudes, values, beliefs and assumptions behind information, and to consider information that uncovers social inequalities and injustices." This approach to education is in stark contrast to the education programs being suggested by some state legislatures which focuses on the "morality" of sexting.

Do Not Criminalize Sexting

No doubt lawmakers are well-intentioned when they push for criminal sexting legislation. But, as many of those lawmakers point out to teens, popularity is a poor substitute for wisdom. Perhaps we adults and professionals too need to take a step back and consider our actions before jumping impulsively into something.

FOURTEEN

Parents Must Take Responsibility for Their Children's Use of Technology

Scott Steinberg

In the following viewpoint Scott Steinberg says that parents are the best defense against a variety of online and technological threats, including sexting. He discusses how today's teens face numerous threats from a myriad of technological devices, including their own cell phones, which they have used to take nude pictures of themselves and send to each other. Sometimes, these pictures end up in the wrong hands, and either get circulated around school or end up on the Internet, where sex offenders and child predators can view them. Steinberg says parents must stay educated about these kinds of threats so they can help their children avoid them. Parents are around their kids most often, have ultimate authority over their devices, and are the best people to talk to their children about difficult and private matters like sex. Therefore, concludes Steinberg, parents are the key to all anti-sexting efforts, and programs to prevent sexting will not work without their help.

Steinberg is a technology consultant who has appeared on major network news programs. He is also the author of The Modern Parent's Guide book series.

How young is too young for a child to have a cell phone?
With the average preschooler now more able to play video games than ride a bike or tie a shoe, and with three-quarters of all middle school– and high school–age kids already owning a phone, it's an increasingly difficult question for today's digital parent to answer.

And it might not even be the most meaningful one.

From growing issues like cyberbullying, cyberbaiting and sexting to rising concerns over Internet safety, cybercrime, and the over-sharing of personal information online, today's family clearly faces a uniquely 21st-century set of digital challenges.

Parents Have a Huge Role to Play

For families in today's rampantly digital world, perhaps the better question is: What are we doing to prepare kids for life in an age of 24/7 connectivity? With 70% of parents believing that schools should do more to educate children about online safety and four-fifths of teachers agreeing that more in-school programs of its type are needed, the answer may be "not nearly enough."

"For parents trying to raise kids and give them the technology to be successful, yet also protect them, there's a sense that no one's there to tell folks what steps to take," said Marian Merritt, Internet safety advocate at Norton. "I hope schools are distributing information and educating (families), but ultimately, parents have a huge role to play (in the process)".

Lack of Involvement Is the Biggest Threat

Today's kids are being trained to use every gadget imaginable but not to consider those devices' extraordinary impact—good and bad—on our lives. Given the speed at which technology moves and how slow parents have been to react, a lot of them must play catchup.

"The biggest threat on the Internet today is parents that are not involved in their children's use of technology," explained Judi Warren, president of Web Wise Kids. "It takes a unified effort to keep kids safe on the Internet (that) has to begin with parents, because it has to start really young."

But laying the responsibility for teaching digital citizenship solely at families' feet would be a mistake, Warren said. "It also has to be a part of ongoing education," she added, noting that kids as young as 2 now commonly use smartphones and other technological devices.

Kids Need Help Navigating New Threats Online

Capable of enlightening nations and empowering individuals, the Web can be an energizing force for good. But with this power comes responsibility.

Consider the meteoric rise of social networks and how they shape our children's experiences. Only six years ago, before Facebook opened to the general public in September 2006, the term "friend" typically described neighborhood pals and school-mates.

Today, it can just as easily reference hundreds of peers, potential crushes or even random strangers. Our kids interact online with these people, some of whom we will never meet.

Of the teens active on these sites, 88% have witnessed acts of meanness or cruelty.

Of course, social networks can also be a perfectly safe and fun way for teens to share ideas and form healthy relationships. It's all in how they're used.

"Lightning can be very dangerous too . . . and you should educate your kids about it," Merritt said. "But it doesn't mean that they're going to be struck by it."

Parents Must Stay Educated

But when it comes to technology's evolving platforms and ethical codes, parents don't always know best. Adults struggle to keep up with the shifting rules of online etiquette and information sharing. And according to a recent study in the online journal *First Monday*, some parents are actively lying to help underage kids

Viewpoint author Scott Steinberg concludes parents are the key to all anti-sexting efforts, and programs to prevent sexting cannot succeed without their help.

join Facebook and other networks, unwittingly exposing them to online bullying.

Alas, no nationally recognized standard or training system exists to teach kids how to navigate the Web. A formalized online-safety course structure and digital-citizenship certification program could be the answer.

Under such a scenario, starting at the pre-K [pre-kindergarten] level, experts would provide hands-on in-school instruction using tablets, touchscreen PCs and Web browsers. Take-home worksheets, online tutorials and interactive activities (delivered via app, downloadable guide or website) could provide added teaching and discussion points for families.

Think Before You Sext

A group of teens age thirteen to nineteen gave multiple reasons they might think twice before sexting.

Question: What are the reasons you would be concerned about sending sexy messages of pictures/video of yourself?*

Answer	Teens (13–19)
Already had a bad experience	6%
Could disappoint family	68%
Could disappoint friends	46%
Could disappoint teacher/coach	38%
Could hurt my relationship or chances with someone I like	63%
Could hurt my reputation	74%
Could hurt my family's reputation	53%
Could get in trouble with the law	46%
Could get in trouble at school	48%
College recruiter might see	43%
Potential (or current) employer might see	51%
Potential embarrassment	77%
Might regret it later	83%
Might make people think I'm slutty in real life	63%
Other	7%
Don't Know	7%

*Answers exceed 100% because respondents were allowed to select multiple answers.

Taken from: National Campaign to Prevent Teen and Unplanned Pregnancy. *Sex and Tech: Results from a Survey of Teens and Young Adults*, 2008.

For parents who want to keep current on Web tools and practices, universities or employers could offer continuing-education classes.

Online forums could connect parents and kids to technology and health-care professionals. And experts could build a database of answers to common tech-safety questions for parents.

That would only be the beginning, however. One logical next step would be creating a network of local chapters capable of providing support for families facing issues like cyberbullying and Web addiction.

The big question is no longer whether these guides will be introduced. Experts say it's simply when.

Parents Are the Key

Stephen Balkam, chief executive officer of the Family Online Safety Institute, encourages creating a holistic "culture of responsibility" when it comes to educating children about Internet safety. Under such a scenario, multiple aspects of society all contribute to keeping kids safe.

Such a program starts at the top, with the government creating laws and providing a safe framework for families. It also includes members of law enforcement doing their part to monitor and catch online predators, Balkam said.

But while educators can stay abreast of Web trends and help guide kids to safety, they can't do it alone. It's ultimately up to parents and their children to maintain running conversations, establish house rules and make wise choices on the Web.

With technology entrenched in our lives, we can no longer afford to simply ignore this. The Internet's potential to improve our kids' lives is boundless. But leaving children, and their parents, unprepared to navigate its pitfalls just doesn't compute.

FIFTEEN

Schools Must Take Responsibility for Preventing Sexting

Mel Riddile

In the following viewpoint Mel Riddile argues that schools must lead in sexting prevention and protection efforts. He thinks it is not unreasonable to ask schools to do this: Schools often protect students from a host of social threats (such as bullying or harassment), and Riddile thinks sexting is no different. Because a lot of issues relating to sexting occur at school or are student body–related, Riddile thinks schools are the first line of defense against such inappropriate conduct. Furthermore, today's digital world means that issues raised at school last well beyond the official school day—educators have a responsibility to follow social problems that develop at school even after the last bell rings, in his opinion. Riddile thinks that schools should work with families to develop appropriate punishments for sexting, but ultimately they must set and enforce their own sexting policies.

A former high school principal, Riddile is the associate director of high school services for the National Association of Secondary School Principals (NASSP).

The *Los Angeles Times* editorial staff believes that kids are naturally mean, and, when they are mean to each other, school officials should mind their own business. "Mean girls—and mean boys—have been terrorizing their classmates since the first schoolhouse was built."

The editorial points out that some courts are refusing to back schools in their efforts to rein in the reputed bad online behavior because it did not occur on school grounds and because the schools failed to prove that the behavior could reasonably be expected or did cause a substantial disruption to the operation of the school.

According to the *Times*, "It isn't just students who are targeted by the online equivalent of "slam books," the notebooks furtively passed around playgrounds in previous generations in which children inscribed insults about their classmates. In Pennsylvania, a student was suspended and shifted to an alternative education program because he posted a parody MySpace profile that described his principal, among other insults, as a "big steroid freak" and a "big whore." A U.S. district judge lifted the suspension, saying that non-disruptive online speech couldn't be punished even if the offensive material could be accessed on school computers."

Schools Must Protect Their Students

If it is my child being victimized, I want school authorities to protect her. If it is someone else's child, she has the right to free speech. I wonder what the *Times* writers would say if it was their child who was the victim of harassment, cyber-bullying, or "sexting?" I bet that they would be contacting their attorney because the school failed to protect their child. The *Times* wants to paint this as schools attempting to extend their authority instead of what this really is—attempts by schools to protect their students and to meet their responsibility for the safety and welfare of the students.

The *Times* assumes that school leaders are power hungry bureaucrats seeking to extend their authority. This is not about authority. The issue here is responsibility. The first responsibility

Educators must make the time and effort to educate themselves about all aspects of sexting and cyberbullying, including its effect on students outside of school, the author contends.

of every principal is to create a warm, safe, and orderly school environment in which students can learn and grow. Principals take their responsibility to protect all students very seriously. They treat their students with the same dignity and respect that they would want for their own child. When one of their students is threatened, harassed, intimidated, or bullied, they act to protect the student because they sincerely care for the student. Failure to do so could be considered negligence. Again we find dedicated, well-intentioned school leaders placed between the proverbial rock and a hard place. If they protect the student, they are violating the perpetrator's rights. If they don't act, they are found negligent.

Educators' Duties Do Not End at 4 P.M.

The editorial supports schools in their effort to prevent harassment and insults only when the behavior occurs on school grounds. Here is the crux of the issue. Where does the responsibility of the school begin and end? Is it, as some districts define, portal-to-portal—from the time the child steps out of the door in the morning until the child arrives home from school? Or, does the responsibility of the school begin and end at the border of school property during school hours? " . . . Educators should recognize the reasonable limits of their authority and confine their discipline to girls and boys who are mean to one another—or to their principal—at school."

I agree with the *Times*, "Schools aren't hermetically sealed off from what students do at home." Today, everyone has an electronic leash (cell phone) that connects them to the entire world. Those electronic signals know no boundaries. If you have a phone, you are connected. As the *Times* correctly points out, "the Internet has eroded an endless number of formerly clear distinctions, including those based on physical location. So, who gets the benefit of the doubt, the schools or the mean boys and girls?

All Schools Need Sexting Policies

First, schools must be safe havens where all students feel physically and emotionally safe and secure at all times.

Schools need clear policies that define harassment, cyberbullying, and "sexting," and they need to consistently enforce the policies. Because the goal is not to apprehend and punish but to deter negative behavior and teach responsible behavior, the policy should contain a prevention component that contains provisions that students be taught "responsible use" of technology.

When considering policies and practices, school officials should put the behaviors into context. Compulsory attendance laws require that students attend school. They have no choice. Unlike a cable TV viewer, students cannot simply change the channel whenever they like. They are compelled to be present and to be subjected to messages that they would normally tune out. Compulsory attendance places an added burden on schools to protect students. For years, one high school allowed students unfettered access to the public address system each morning. The simple act of standing in line allowed any student who wished to say anything about any subject. Not only did the morning announcements go on forever, but the entire school was forcibly subjected to frequent, inane rants. The new principal recognized his responsibility to all students by placing a staff member in charge of the announcements, which required prior approval and were delivered by trained student government officers.

An enforceable school policy is not a board policy that passes the buck to the principal by simply stating that the school should have a policy. This provides board members with cover and wiggle room when parents complain, but it places school leaders in a position to have the rug pulled out from under them at any time that a constituent or board member disagrees. The result is usually an unenforceable policy.

Electronic Behavior Should Be No Different

Schools would not allow anyone to print and freely distribute paper flyers that contained nude pictures, threats, or slanderous statements, nor should they permit those behaviors simply because they occur electronically.

Schools must recognize that the Internet gives every student a license to print. A cell phone is literally an electronic printing press that sends messages to the entire world with the touch of a button. As such, the consequences of misdirected or inappropriate messages are instantaneous and virtually limitless in scope. In other words, one message can move faster and do a lot more damage than the printed word. One student with a cell phone can literally direct a "reign of terror" toward another student.

At some level, students understand that electronic messages are impossible to stop and can be viewed by anyone. Consequently, they are quicker to anger and easily incited to violence when someone posts a derogatory message on social networking sites

To Whom Do Young People Send Sexually Explicit Pictures?

An MTV/Associated Press survey asked fourteen- to twenty-one-year-olds who admitted to sexting to whom they sent pictures, and what they thought happened to them.

Question: To whom did you send naked pictures of yourself?*

Answer	Percentage
My boyfriend or girlfriend	59%
My husband, wife, or significant other	18%
Someone I had a crush on	11%
Someone I dated or hooked up with	24%
Someone I just met	5%
Someone I wanted to date or hook up with	18%
A good friend	11%
Someone I know, not a good friend	4%
Someone I only knew online and had never met in person	10%

Question: As far as you know, did the person you shared the naked pictures you took of yourself share the pictures with anybody else without your permission, or do you not think they did that?

Answer	Percentage
They shared them with someone else	9%
I do not think they shared them with anyone else	77%
Not sure	12%
Refused to answer	3%

Question: Did you ever share any naked pictures or videos that someone sent you with another person, or not?

Answer	Percentage
I have shared naked pictures or videos that someone sent me with another person	18%
I have never done this	82%

*Answers exceed 100% because respondents were allowed to select multiple answers.

Taken from: National Campaign to Prevent Teen and Unplanned Pregnancy. *Sex and Tech: Results from a Survey of Teens and Young Adults,* 2008.

such as Facebook or MySpace. Some schools even refer to the resulting altercations as "MySpace fights" or "Facebook fights."

Harassment is harassment whether it is electronic, verbal, or in print.

Schools Must Work with Families

Problems usually stem from how schools deal with the issues not from the fact they actually address the issue. Because most parents don't want a suspension on their child's record and certainly not a cyber violation, making suspension from school the first response will set everyone up for a disagreement. Attempting to use school authority to force someone to "take down" a comment or an inappropriate post will, more often than not, result in a confrontation. Many principals have found success by simply having a conversation with the parents of the offender. In my experience, the simple act of setting up a meeting almost always resulted in successful resolution because, it turns out, the parents were not aware that their child's electronic behavior in the first place.

If a student brought a *Playboy* to school in the 1970s, I confiscated the magazine and called the parents. Future violations would result in strict disciplinary action. Distributing inappropriate photographs of students would result in the same. In the case of "sexting," schools must make it clear in writing that this behavior is harmful, probably illegal, and unacceptable.

Any student who is bullied, harassed or "sexted" has been victimized. The behavior should be treated as serious and stopped. The victimized student should be given support from a student-services team consisting of an administrator, counselor, social worker, and a school psychologist.

Like any other illegal acts, these behaviors should be reported to the School Resource Officer or the appropriate law enforcement personnel. Child abuse must be reported to the appropriate authorities in a timely manner. This should be explicitly stated in policy.

Schools must have clear guidelines and policies that allow them to deal internally with bullying, intimidation, harassment, and "sexting," separate and apart from any criminal or legal action.

SIXTEEN

Technology Can Help Prevent Teen Sexting

Rushworth M. Kidder

In the following viewpoint Rushworth M. Kidder laments that Americans have let technology inform their morals and ethics, rather than letting their morals and ethics guide their use of technology. The result is the sexting phenomenon, in which young people take nude pictures of themselves and send them to others, with sometimes disastrous results. Kidder is disappointed that more people did not see this dangerous trend coming, given their general unthinking use of technology and society's obsession with sex. He suggests one way to curb sexting is to design a program that sends a copy of a texted picture to a parent or guardian. He recognizes the ethical problems that might be raised by such a program but thinks this would help young people make better choices and open up discussions about the issue with their parents. Kidder concludes that rather than being surprised that technology has created new problems like sexting, humans should use their ethics to anticipate such problems and use technology ethically and smartly.

Before his death in 2012, Kidder was a university professor, *Christian Science Monitor* columnist, and the founder of the Institute for Global Ethics.

Rushworth M. Kidder, "Sexting and Our Moral Failure," Institute for Global Ethics, April 20, 2009. Copyright © 2009 by the Institute for Global Ethics. All rights reserved. Reproduced by permission.

You'd think we would have foreseen it. Give a kid a cell-phone camera, and we know they'll take pictures. Give them messaging capability, and we know they'll start texting messages and sending photos of themselves to each other—alone or with friends, goofy or serious.

Then why didn't it occur to us that some of those shots would be in the nude?

The author thinks that if technology can be used for sexting, technology can also be used to prevent it as well.

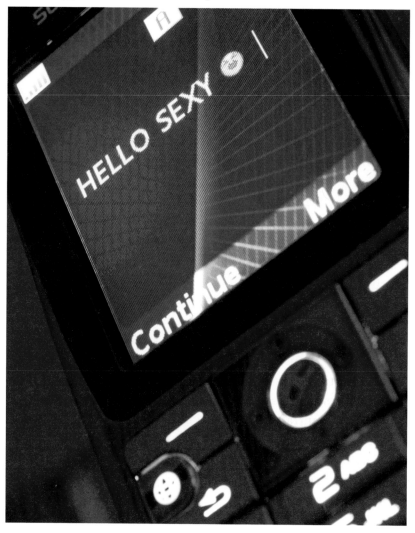

When Technology Informs Our Morals

Once again we've been caught flat-footed by the latest teen fad: sexting. According to a survey last fall [in 2008] by the National Campaign to Prevent Teen and Unplanned Pregnancy, 20 percent of teens say they have sent or posted nude or seminude pictures or videos of themselves.

This isn't the first time our lack of moral futurism has tripped us up. Several years ago it was DWT—driving while texting. Only when DWT created headlines with the death of five teenage girls in upstate New York in June 2007—and then, spectacularly, in the Los Angeles commuter train wreck that killed 25 people last September—did we begin to understand that it could be fatal.

Shame on texting drivers and teenage sexters? Sure. But shame on us as well. We regularly let our technologies leverage our ethics, so that single unethical acts can create enormous, unforeseen ethical problems. Then we act surprised when fads or calamities strike. "Wow!" we say. "Technology has created a whole new ethical problem! Who knew?"

We knew—or at least we should have. Here we've got these cell-phone cameras. Here we live in a video culture drenched with explicit eroticism. Here we access an Internet system where pornography is the single most common target of Web searches. How hard would it have been to imagine what would happen if you put these three threads into the hands of teenagers with little instruction and no warnings?

The Many Reasons to Avoid Sexting

What's wrong with sexting? For starters, here are seven arguments:

- It constitutes the kind of "lewd and lascivious behavior" that society seeks to avoid and the law generally prohibits.
- When you transmit such images, you may be guilty of circulating pornography—a tough charge, especially when it involves minors and could lead to permanent labeling as a criminal sex offender.
- Sexting surrenders a key aspect of your individuality—the way you invite others to see you—to a medium beyond your

control. What keeps recipients from forwarding your picture to dozens of others—or posting it for everyone everywhere to see?

- Sexting may encourage aggressive sexual activity that, absent responsibility or affection, is especially harmful to young minds and bodies.
- Sexting promotes a desensitized peer culture where sexual activity becomes more difficult to resist—even among teens who avoid instant gratification and value abstinence.
- If such a culture leads to teen pregnancy and abortion—or early marriages at high risk of divorce, generating more single-parent families—the psychic and financial burdens to society can be severe.
- If such a culture leads to rape, domestic abuse, and sexual predation, the consequences are enormous.

What should we do? The Vermont Senate recently passed and its House is now [in 2009] considering legislation that, oddly enough, *reduces* the penalties for sexting. Supporters on both sides of the aisle explain that they aren't *legalizing* sexting so much as partially *decriminalizing* it. Why? Because after 12-year-old Brooke Bennett was sexually assaulted and murdered in Vermont last summer, the legislature crafted one of the nation's toughest sexual predator laws. The proposed sexting law, its supporters argue, would merely ensure that juveniles caught sending these pictures won't be subject to punishment under that toughened law. They could still be prosecuted under pornography or lewd-behavior statutes, but they wouldn't be placed on sex-offender registries for the rest of their lives.

Fair enough. Young people making stupid mistakes deserve reformation, not retribution. But how?

What if Technology Could Help?

Here's an idea: What if cell phones came equipped with a feature that, whenever *any* picture was sent or received, would automatically send a copy to a designated third party? Some parents wouldn't use it, trusting their teens. Others would have

Sexting Occurs on Multiple Platforms

Most teens who sext take and receive sexually explicit photos of themselves via text messages, but other technology—such as social networking or instant messaging—is sometimes involved.*

Technology used	Respondent appeared in or created image	Respondent received image
Social networking site	5%	8%
Text messaging	44%	56%
Cell phone camera/cell phone	21%	26%
Instant messaging	10%	6%
Digital/video camera	21%	2%

*Answers exceed 100% because participants were allowed to select more than one answer.

Taken from: Kimberly J. Mitchell et al. "Prevalence and Characteristics of Youth Sexting: A National Study." *Pediatrics*, vol. 129, no. 1, January 2012, p. 52.

the pictures sent to an archive to access later if they suspected something. Still others would have the pictures sent directly to their own cell phone in real time. Whatever they did, parents would have to make a choice about whether to have that feature permanently turned on or not. And that choice would compel a conversation about sexting with their teens. "Tell me why you want the feature turned off," parents could say. "If you're only sending or getting innocent pictures, having it on won't bother you. But if you plan on sexting—sorry, I'm not paying for your phone."

Not every parent would opt in, and some teens might buy their own phones. But every would-be sexter would have to suspect that *some* parents would have access. Would he or she (and most sexters are female) be so quick to send pictures?

Let Our Ethics Inform Our Technology Use

Whatever the result, the very availability of such a feature would raise a tough moral dilemma, pitting the rights of teenage privacy against the responsibilities of adult supervision. We don't want censorship, but we also don't want pornography. If every parent's purchase of a phone for a teen would provide the occasion for a serious ethical conversation on that point, we'd be well on our way to addressing sexting. Then, instead of technology leveraging our ethics, we might find that our ethical foresight was beginning to drive our use of technology.

What You Should Know About Sexting

According to the *Sex and Tech* survey by the National Campaign to Prevent Teen and Unplanned Pregnancy and CosmoGirl.com, the following statistics were reported by those surveyed:

- Twenty percent of teens aged 13 to 19 have electronically sent, or posted online, nude or seminude pictures or video of themselves.
- Twenty-two percent of teen girls aged 13 to 19 have done this.
- Eighteen percent of teen boys aged 13 to 19 have done this.
- Eleven percent of young teen girls (aged 13 to 16) have done this.
- Thirty-three percent of young adults (aged 20 to 26) have done this.
- Thirty-six percent of young adult women (aged 20 to 26) have done this.
- Thirty-one percent of young adult men (aged 20 to 26) have done this.
- Thirty-nine percent of all teens, 37 percent of teen girls and 40 percent of teen boys say they have received sexually suggestive text, e-mail, or IM messages.
- Fifty-nine percent of all young adults, 56 percent of young adult women and 62 percent of young adult men say they have received sexually suggestive text, e-mail, or IM messages.

- Seventy-one percent of teen girls and 67 percent of teen guys who have sent or posted sexually suggestive content say they did so to a boyfriend/girlfriend.
- Twenty-one percent of teen girls and 39 percent of teen boys said they sent such content to someone they wanted to date or hook up with.
- Fifteen percent of teens who have sent or posted nude/semi-nude images of themselves say they have done so to someone they only knew online.
- Thirty-six percent of teen girls and 39 percent of teen boys say it is common for nude or seminude photos to get shared with people other than the intended recipient.
- Forty-seven percent of teens (and 38 percent of young adults) say "pressure from guys" is a reason girls and women send and post sexually suggestive messages and images.
- Twenty-four percent of teens (and 20 percent of young adults) say "pressure from friends" is a reason guys send and post sexually suggestive messages and images.

According to the Digital Abuse Survey taken by MTV and the Associated Press, the following statistics were reported:
- Twenty-four percent of 14- to 17-year-olds report some involvement in sexting.
- Thirty-three percent of 18- to 24-year-olds had some such involvement.
- Ten percent of 14- to 24-year-olds have sent a sexual image.
- Twenty-four percent sent the image to someone they wanted to hook up with.
- Twenty-nine percent sent the image to someone they only knew online.
- Sixty-one percent of those who sent an image said they had been pressured by someone else to do so.

According to a national survey of teens aged twelve to seventeen by the Pew Internet and American Life Project, the following statistics were reported:

- Four percent of teens said they had sent sexually suggestive nude or nearly nude images of themselves to someone else via text messaging.
- Fifteen percent of teens said they had received sexually suggestive nude or nearly nude images.
- Eight percent of 17-year-olds had sent such images.
- Thirty percent had received such images.

Researchers at the University of New Hampshire published the following information about sexting in a 2012 report:

- Of youth aged ten to seventeen, 2.5 percent had appeared in or created nude or nearly nude pictures or videos.
- One percent had appeared in or created sexually explicit photos.
- Of youth surveyed, 7.1 percent said they had received nude or nearly nude images of others; 5.9 percent said they had received sexually explicit images; and 9.6 percent reported appearing in, creating, or receiving sexually suggestive images.

According to a study by researchers at the University of Rhode Island, the following statistics were reported:

- Fifty-six percent of all college students have received sexually suggestive images via text messaging.
- Seventy-eight percent have received suggestive messages.
- Sixty-seven percent of students have sent sexually suggestive messages.
- Seventy-three percent of the messages were sent to a relationship partner.
- Ten percent were sent without consent of the person who had originally sent the message.

What You Should Do About Sexting

The best way to avoid the consequences that come from sexting is to avoid engaging in it entirely. Do not send pictures of yourself to others; do not forward pictures you receive to anyone else. Of course, that is easier said than done. A good way to help yourself understand sexting's damaging reach is to picture—really visualize—what it would feel like to have others view such a photo of you. How would you feel if your mother or father saw it? Your siblings? Your grandparents, teachers, or coaches? How would you feel if it were projected on a huge screen in your school's auditorium? Posted on Facebook? Printed on thousands of fliers and strewn around your school? Printed on T-shirts? Plastered on the evening news? All of these scenarios are possible once a digital image leaves your device.

The Pressure to Sext

What many adults do not yet understand about sexting is that it often occurs under enormous social pressure. Although some young people volunteer to send pictures of themselves without much prodding, others are heavily coerced into doing so. One study conducted by MTV and the Associated Press, for example, found that 61 percent of all young people who have sent or received nude pictures said they felt pressured to do so. Some teens feel compelled to sext pictures to prove they are cool, to keep a boyfriend or girlfriend interested, to prove that they are heterosexual, and to avoid being socially isolated or called cruel and degrading names.

Peer pressure is a difficult part of life when you are young. It is unfortunate that you can now add sexting to the list of behaviors you may face pressure from your peers to engage in, such as drinking, using drugs, skipping school, or dressing or talking a certain way. It takes a self-confident, strong, and self-assured person to resist peer pressure in all its forms. Know that you will feel best about yourself if you do not give into the pressure to sext.

Ways to Avoid Sexting

Because it is sometimes hard to just say no, there are a variety of excuses or coping strategies you might employ to get out of sexting. Researchers at the National Society for the Prevention of Cruelty to Children conducted extensive interviews with a variety of middle school and high school students to learn how they coped with the pressure to sext. Some survived the pressure by developing impressive mechanisms and excuses. One thirteen-year-old girl named Jodie, for example, describes how she used a roundabout, bait-and-switch technique to avoid a boy's request to send a nude photo of herself:

> Some boy asked me, "Can I have a picture of you," I was like, "My display picture" and he was like "No I mean a special photo" and I was like, "What special photo[?]" and he was like, "Like you in your bra" and I was like "No," and I was like, "I have one of me in my bikini" And he was like, "can you send it anyway" and I was like, "[my cousin] Kaycee's got it" because he knows my cousin. And then them two went to the same school, so I was like, "you can ask her to send it" and then I was like, "Kaycee, delete the photo and don't send it to him." Like when you say no to people, like you fall out with them, so I just make excuses.[1]

In another instance, Jodie told a boy who requested a photo that she could not give him one because the terms of her cell phone contract limited the amount of data she was able to send:

> He was like, "Oh you are so cute" and I was like, "You are random" and he was like, . . . "You are, can you send me a picture" and then I was like, "No I don't have any credit to send you it" and . . . then he is like, "Yeah it's free over BBM [BlackBerry Messenger]" and I was like because I'm on contract it costs me money. And he is like, "Okay then."[2]

Other strategies could include telling someone who requests a photo that your parents monitor all of your text messages. Some parents ask to see their children's cell phones at least once a day;

others confiscate them in the evenings. Someone trying to pressure you into sending a photo might say, "Just delete the photo after you send it, so your parents won't find it on your phone." But there now exist numerous sophisticated monitoring programs that parents can subscribe to, even without their child's knowledge. UKnowKids is one example of a parental monitoring service that lets parents know how many text messages their children have sent and received, whether these include pictures, the time and date such messages were sent or received, the name and phone number of the sender and receiver, and other detailed information. For example, your parents might know you sent a picture message to Josh Evans at 11:34 P.M.—should they ask to see it and you have deleted it, it will certainly arouse suspicion. It can be easier to tell someone who is hounding you for a photo that your parents monitor all of your messages, and it is just not worth getting into trouble for. No matter what solution you devise for avoiding a person's request to sext a photo, once you find a way to say no, you will feel in control of your present and future: a powerful and satisfying feeling.

Finally, never forward a compromising photo to others. Should you ever receive one, delete it immediately. Think about the way you would feel if it were a photo of your sister, your brother, or your best friend. Feel the responsibility to protect people who were not able to protect themselves. Let the parade of shame and ridicule end with you by choosing to not participate in the humiliation and degradation of others.

If appealing to your sense of ethics is not enough to convince you to not forward pictures from others, know that in some states, it is a crime to distribute sexually explicit or otherwise indecent photos of minors. Texting nude or partially nude photos of others are included. Penalties range from fines to jail time to suspension or expulsion from school to being forced to register as a sex offender. In all cases, it is best to delete any materials you may receive so as not to implicate yourself in any of the legal or punitive repercussions surrounding sexting.

Notes

1. Quoted in Jessica Ringrose, Rosalind Gill, Sonia Livingstone, and Laura Harvey, "A Qualitative Study of Children, Young People, and 'Sexting,'" National Society for the Prevention of Cruelty to Children, 2012. www.nspcc.org.uk/Inform /resourcesforprofessionals/sexualabuse/sexting-research-report _wdf89269.pdf.
2. Quoted in Ringrose et al., "A Qualitative Study."

ORGANIZATIONS TO CONTACT

The editors have compiled the following list of organizations concerned with the issues debated in this book. The descriptions are derived from materials provided by the organizations. All have publications or information available for interested readers. The list was compiled on the date of publication of the present volume; names, addresses, phone and fax numbers, and e-mail and Internet addresses may change. Be aware that many organizations take several weeks or longer to respond to inquiries, so allow as much time as possible.

Berkman Center for Internet & Society
Harvard University
23 Everett St., 2nd Fl.
Cambridge, MA 02138
(617) 495-7547
e-mail: cyber@law.harvard.edu
website: http://cyber.law.harvard.edu

Founded in 1997, the center is dedicated to the study of the Internet and its effects on politics, law, and culture. Among its many projects is Digital Natives, which studies the Internet use of a generation "born digital"; that is, young people who have been using and creating digital media all their lives. Numerous publications and fact sheets about sexting can be retrieved from its website.

Center for Safe and Responsible Internet Use
474 W. Twenty-Ninth Ave.
Eugene, OR 97405
(541) 556-1145
e-mail: contact@csriu.org
website: www.cyberbully.org

The center was founded in 2002 by Nancy Willard, an expert on student Internet use management in schools and the author of

Cyberbullying and Cyberthreats. In addition to briefs and guides for educators and parents, the center offers numerous reports, articles, and books for student researchers, including "Sexting and Youth" and *Cyber-Safe Kids, Cyber-Savvy Teens.* The site also offers a social networking code for young people called the DigiDesiderata, with rules such as "If you compare your profile and number of friends with others, you may mistakenly think you are 'hot' or 'not.' Seek quality, not quantity, in your online friending."

Consortium for School Networking (CoSN)
1025 Vermont Ave. NW, Ste. 1010
Washington, DC 20005
(202) 861-2676; toll-free: (866) 267-8747
website: www.cosn.org

Founded in 1992, CoSN is a nonprofit organization that advocates and develops ways of using Internet technologies to improve teaching and learning in kindergarten through twelfth grade (K–12). It supports the use of open-source software in schools to foster collaboration and to allow teachers to modify and share their applications. The center publishes reports such as *Hot Technologies for K–12 Schools* and "Web 2.0 in Education," which argues that schools must integrate social networking and participatory media or be left behind. Some of its publications address sexting and related issues.

Crisis Intervention Center
5603 S. Fourteenth St.
Fort Smith, AR 72901
(479) 782-1821 • hotline: (800) 359-0056
website: www.crisisinterventioncenter.org

The mission statement of Crisis Intervention Center is to end domestic violence and sexual assault. Recognizing that sexting has resulted in sexual assault, bullying, and suicide, the center offers information and fact sheets related to sexting and a hotline teens can call should they feel overwhelmed by the issue.

Electronic Frontier Foundation (EFF)
454 Shotwell St., San Francisco, CA 94110-1914
(415) 436-9333
e-mail: information@eff.org
website: www.eff.org

The EFF is an organization of students and other individuals that aims to promote a better understanding of telecommunications issues. It fosters awareness of civil liberties issues arising from advancements in computer-based communications media and supports litigation to preserve, protect, and extend First Amendment rights in computing and telecommunications technologies. Some of its publications address sexting and related issues; most take the stance that sexting has been hyped by the media and is not a serious problem.

Enough Is Enough
746 Walker Rd., Ste. 116
Great Falls, VA 22066
(703) 476-7890
website: www.internetsafety101.org

Enough Is Enough: Protecting Our Children Online is a group that fights online pornography, child pornography, child stalking, sexual predation, and other forms of online victimization. As part of its Internet Safety campaign, it condemns sexting and teaches young people to use technology responsibly and defensively.

Internet Education Foundation
Center for Democracy and Technology
1634 Eye St. NW, Ste. 1100
Washington, DC 20006
(202) 638-4370
e-mail: tim@neted.org
website: www.neted.org

Founded in 1996, the foundation is a nonprofit public interest group that works to educate and lobby policy makers and legislators in support of free expression and privacy in web technologies.

It supports "net neutrality" laws: government regulation of broadband providers to keep them from controlling online "traffic" in an unfair way—for example, by favoring some kinds of transmissions or content over others. Website links include GetNetWise, a toolkit of video tutorials and up-to-date blog posts such as "Are Teens Broadcasting Their Mobile Location on Facebook?," and "A New Social Networking Resource for Families."

Kaiser Family Foundation
1330 G St. NW
Washington, DC 20005
(202) 347-5270
website: www.kff.org

The foundation is a nonprofit research organization focusing on health care issues. It also serves as a clearinghouse of public health information in the United States. Its Media and Health site offers the 2010 report *Generation M²: Media in the Lives of 8- to 18-Year-Olds*, a comprehensive national survey that charts the rise and effects of social media use among American youth from 1999 through 2009. Other useful resources available on its website include the report "The Teen Media Juggling Act: Media Multitasking Among American Youth."

National Center for Bullying Prevention
PACER Center
8161 Normandale Blvd.
Bloomington, MN 55437
toll-free: (888) 248-0822
website: www.pacer.org/bullying

Funded by the US Department of Education's Office of Special Education Programs, the center is an advocate for children with disabilities and all children subjected to bullying, from elementary through high school. Bullying prevention resources (available in English, Spanish, Hmong, and Somali) include video clips, reading lists, creative writing exercises, group activities, and numerous downloadable handouts such as "Bullying Fast Facts." The center sponsors school and community workshops and events such as National Bullying Awareness Week each October. Many of its materials address sexting-related bullying.

Wired Safety
1 Bridge St.
Irvington-on-Hudson, NY 10533
(201) 463-8663
e-mail: parry@aftab.com
websites: www.wiredsafety.org; www.stopcyberbullying.org

Wired Safety is an Internet safety and help group that offers articles, activities, and advice designed for seven- to seventeen-year-olds on a range of issues, including cyberbullying, cyber stalking, and harassment, that stem from sexting and other sources. Resources include a Cyber911 Help Line, a cyberstalking poll, cyberbullying Q&As, and a speakers bureau. Information available on the websites covers Facebook privacy protection, how to handle sexting, building safe websites, and many other topics. Wired Safety also sponsors the annual WiredKids Summit on Capitol Hill; in a role reversal, tech-savvy teens get the chance to present cyber-safety research, raise cyberbullying issues, and tell industry and government leaders what they need to know about cyber safety.

BIBLIOGRAPHY

Books

Sameer Hinduja and Justin W. Patchin, *School Climate 2.0: Preventing Cyberbullying and Sexting One Classroom at a Time.* Thousand Oaks, CA: Corwin, 2012.

Brenda Hunter and Kristen Blair, *From Santa to Sexting: Helping Your Child Safely Navigate Middle School and Shape the Choices That Last a Lifetime.* Abilene, TX: Leafwood, 2012.

Matt Ivester, lol . . .OMG!: *What Every Student Needs to Know About Online Reputation Management, Digital Citizenship and Cyberbullying.* Seattle: CreateSpace Independent Publishing Platform, 2011.

Robin M. Kowalski, Susan P. Limber, and Patricia W. Agatston, *Cyberbullying: Bullying in the Digital Age.* Hoboken, NJ: Wiley-Blackwell, 2012.

Kay Stephens and Vinitha Nair, *Cyberslammed: Understand, Prevent, Combat and Transform the Most Common Cyberbullying Tactics.* Rockland, ME: sMashup, 2012.

Periodicals and Internet Sources

American Civil Liberties Union of Ohio, "Sexting," 2011. www .acluohio.org/issues/juvenilejustice/SextingPositionSheet.pdf.

Austin (TX) Statesman, "Give Parents, Authorities, Teens Tools to Deal with Sexting," February 10, 2011. www.statesman .com/opinion/give-parents-authorities- teens-tools-to-deal -with-1243887.html.

Carl Bialik, "Sexting, an Epidemic of Fuzzy Math," *Wall Street Journal*, April 8, 2009. http://online.wsj.com/article /SB123913888769898347.html.

Nicole Brady, "Law on Sexting Leaves Our Teens Dangerously Exposed," *Age* (Australia), June 2, 2012. www.theage.com .au/opinion/politics/the-law-on- sexting-leaves-our-teens -dangerously-exposed-20120603-1zq0q.html.

Tracy Clark-Flory, "The New Pornographers," *Salon*, February 20, 2009. www.salon.com/2009/02/20/sexting_teens/.

Express-Times (Lehigh Valley, PA) "Find the Right Punishment for Teen-Age 'Sexting,'" January 27, 2011. www.lehighval leylive.com/today/index.ssf/2011/01/opinion_find_the_right _punishm.html.

David M. Hall, "What the Tragedy of Tyler Clementi Teaches About Teen Sexting," CNN.com, March 19, 2012. http://ina merica.blogs.cnn.com/2012/03/19/opinion-what-the-tragedy -of-tyler- clementi-teaches-about-teen-sexting/.

Joshua D. Herman, "Sexting: It's No Joke, It's a Crime," *Illinois Bar Journal*, April 2010. www.isba.org/ibj/2010/04/sextingits nojokeitsacrime.

Jan Hoffman, "Poisoned Web: A Girl's Nude Photos, and Altered Lives," *New York Times*, March 26, 2011. www.nytimes .com/2011/03/27/us/27sexting.html?ref=us .

Jan Hoffman, "States Struggle with Minors' Sexting," *New York Times*, March 26, 2011. www.nytimes.com/2011/03/27/us /27sextinglaw.html.

William Jackson, "Sexting and Bullying One in the Same," *Florida Times-Union* (Jacksonville, FL), October 26, 2011. http://jacksonville.com/opinion/blog/400553/william-jack son/2011-10-26/sexting-and-bullying-one-same.

Jeff A. Katz, "Warning: The Dangers of Sexting," *Huffington Post*, March 1, 2010. www.huffingtonpost.com/jeff-a-katz/warning -the-dangers-of-se_b_481179.html.

Nick Lacroce, "The Young and the Sexting: The Punishment Should Better Fit the Crime," *Patriot News* (Central Pennsylvania), October 18, 2009. www.pennlive.com/edito rials/index.ssf/2009/10/the_young_and_the_sexting_the.html.

Robert Nelson, "Teen Sexting's Main Danger Lies in Adult Overreaction," *Age* (Australia), July 12, 2011. www.theage .com.au/opinion/society-and- culture/teen-sextings-main-dan ger-lies-in-adult-overreaction-20110711-lhal9.html.

Clem Newton-Brown, "Risky Sexting by Teens Doesn't Necessarily Make Them Child Pornographers," *Age* (Australia), May 8, 2012. www.theage.com.au/opinion/politics/risky -sexting-by-teens-doesnt- necessarily-make-them-child-por nographers-20120507-ly8zj.html.

Dennis O'Reilly, "The Love Letter, Devolved: A Sexting Revolution," *Badger Herald* (University of Wisconsin–Madison), October 1, 2010. http://badgerherald.com/oped/2010/10/01 /the_love_letter_devo.php.

Jenna Price, "Wrong Number? Sexting in the Spotlight," *Canberra Times* (Australia), April 24, 2012. www.canberra times.com.au/opinion/wrong- number-sexting-in-the-spot light-20120424-lxi3v.html.

Andrea Cornell Salavy, "Should 'Sexting' Be Decriminalized?," *Atlanta Journal Constitution*, April 24, 2009. http://blogs.ajc .com/woman/2009/04/24/should- sexting-be-decriminalized/.

Christopher Shea, "Is Sexting Constitutional?," *Boston Globe*, April 28, 2010. www.boston.com/bostonglobe/ideas/brainiac /2010/04/is_sexting_cons.html.

Paul Wallis, "Australia's Anti Sexting Campaign—$120 Million for What?," *Digital Journal*, April 15, 2011. http://digitaljour nal.com/article/305682.

Websites

A Thin Line (www.athinline.org). This site is run by an MTV campaign against sexting, cyberbullying, and digital dating abuse. It contains inspirational stories from celebrities, interest-ing videos, and advice regarding sexting and other digital issues.

Connect Safely (www.connectsafely.org). This website is for par-ents, teens, educators, advocates, and others. It offers informative news articles on sexting and advice for both parents and teens on the issue.

Cyberbullying Research Center (http://cyberbullying.us/). This site is run by two cyberbullying experts, Sameer Hinduja and Justin Patchin, both of whom write prolifically on the problem of cyberbullying. It offers up-to-date information about the nature, extent, causes, and consequences of cyberbullying among adolescents. It features numerous articles, fact sheets, polls, surveys, and other useful materials on sexting.

Family Online Safety Institute's Safety Contract (www.fosi.org /images/stories/resources/family-online-safety- contract.pdf). This contract, published by the Family Online Safety Institute, provides a starting point for teens and their parents to discuss safety and technology issues. Students should feel free to add a clause about sexting to the contract, which covers texting, Internet use, social media, and other issues.

National Conference on State Legislatures Sexting Legislation page (www.ncsl.org/issues-research/telecom/sexting-legislation-2012.aspx). This useful and authoritative source contains the most up-to-date state laws regarding sexting.

NetSmartz (www.netsmartz.org). This site, run by the National Center for Missing and Exploited Children, seeks to educate youth and adults on the dangers of various digital behaviors, including sexting. A special section for teens offers real-life stories, inspirational and informative videos, and a helpline where teens can turn if they are having trouble.

INDEX

Pew Internet & American Life Project, 26, 78
Phippen, Andy, 32
Pittsburgh (PA) *Post-Gazette* (newspaper), 69–70
Polls. *See* Surveys

R
Race, prevalence of sexting by, 23
Rapoport, Paul, 14
Riascos, Leslie, 22
Rice, David, 10–11
Riddile, Mel, 90
Ringrose, Jessica, 37

S
Schwarzbaum, Lisa, 58
Sexting
  adults overreact to, 15–18
  adults should worry about, 9–13
  considerable numbers of teens engage in, 19–23
  inclusion of term in dictionary, 5, 6
  is less common among teens than thought, 24–28
  is not valid form of teen self-expression, 66–71
  is valid form of teen self-expression, 60–65
  laws on, by state, *81*
  no trustworthy statistics on prevalence exist, 29–36
  peer pressure causes, 37–43

  prevalence among teens, *11, 22, 25–26, 27,* 67, 69, 99
  primal exhibitionism causes, 44–49
  results from normal teen sexual expression, 50–54
  schools must take responsibility for preventing, 90–96
  sex-crazed culture of US promotes, 55–59
  should be a crime, 72–75
  should not be a crime, 51–52, 54, 76–83
  technologies used for, *101*
  technology can help prevent teen, 97–102
Skumanick, George, 61
Smith, Dick, 20
Stael, Germaine de, 45
Steinberg, Scott, 84
Suicides, due to sexting, 5, 69
  are not the norm, 78–80
Surveys
  on characteristics of sexted pictures, 46
  on concerns teens have about sexting, 88
  on handling of sexting cases in Ohio, 74–75
  on sexting, sample size/definition of "sexting" in, *33*
  of sexting among Houston high school students, 22–23
  on teen sexting, *42,* 78, *95, 99*